Alan St. Aubyn

**The junior Dean**

Vol. III

Alan St. Aubyn

**The junior Dean**
*Vol. III*

ISBN/EAN: 9783337051013

Printed in Europe, USA, Canada, Australia, Japan

Cover: Foto ©ninafisch / pixelio.de

More available books at **www.hansebooks.com**

# THE JUNIOR DEAN

A Novel

By ALAN St. AUBYN

AUTHOR OF 'A FELLOW OF TRINITY'

IN THREE VOLUMES
VOL. III.

London
CHATTO & WINDUS, PICCADILLY
1891

# CONTENTS OF VOL. III.

| CHAPTER | | PAGE |
|---|---|---|
| XXVII. AN UNPLEASANT INTERVIEW | - | 1 |
| XXVIII. A CAMBRIDGE SCANDAL | - | 25 |
| XXIX. RUSTICATED | - | 43 |
| XXX. JACK GOES DOWN | - | 69 |
| XXXI. A DEBATE AT NEWNHAM | - | 85 |
| XXXII. A WINTER NIGHT'S TALE | - | 104 |
| XXXIII. GOOD-BYE! | - | 117 |
| XXXIV. A SAD HOME-COMING | - | 135 |
| XXXV. THAT LITTLE BILL | - | 160 |
| XXXVI. DARK DAYS | - | 184 |
| XXXVII. 'O, ABSALOM, MY SON, MY SON!' | - | 204 |
| XXXVIII. ALONE IN THE WORLD | - | 225 |
| XXXIX. MOLLY'S QUIXOTISM | - | 247 |
| XL. A RIFT IN THE CLOUDS | - | 268 |

# THE JUNIOR DEAN

## CHAPTER XXVII.

AN UNPLEASANT INTERVIEW.

THE porter of St. Stephen's had had his dinner, and he was taking a nap after it. He was not accustomed to being disturbed in this post-prandial observance. He usually slept all the afternoon (the college ale was the strongest in the 'Varsity), but to-day he was disturbed before he'd had forty winks.

The interruption took the form of a lady; the same lady that he had shown to the Junior Dean's rooms in the morning.

The fog had cleared now, and a wan wintry sunshine feebly lighted up the court.

'I am sorry to disturb you,' said the lady, 'but I can't find the rooms I am looking for. It was so foggy when you took me there this morning that I cannot remember the way.'

She was dressed so differently this afternoon that for a few moments the porter did not recognise her. She was richly dressed, and wore a hat with feathers—a very becoming hat, with long curling feathers that got mixed up with her fluffy yellow hair in a quite bewildering way; and she carried a bag—a sealskin bag that matched her jacket—a jaunty bag that adapted itself to a muff; a jaunty jacket edged with fur; a jaunty hat, and a rich dress with trailing skirts that made a delightful *frou-frou* whisper run round the court as she passed through it.

The men going down to the boats passed

her in the quad, and with one accord turned round and looked after her. It was like a vision of May Week. It was like the Queen of Sheba going up that musty old college staircase.

There was no one in the Junior Dean's room, and it was a quarter to three o'clock.

The porter met the Junior Dean in the quad as he was going back to the lodge.

'A lady in your rooms, sir,' he said, touching his hat.

'Ah!' said the Junior Dean, 'thank you,' and he limped hurriedly across the court with a tender smile on his face. He was thinking of Molly.

'The same lady that called this morning, sir,' said the man, calling after him. The Junior Dean paused, stopped, and then limped slowly back; but the light had quite died out of his face.

'I — I can't see this lady just now,

Wilkins,' he said, speaking with an effort; and his lip twitched in that nervous fashion that showed he was moved. 'Will you tell her that—that I am engaged; that I cannot see her now? If she has any message, perhaps she will write.'

He turned his back on his own rooms, and hurried across the court to another staircase. It was the senior tutor's staircase, and he was in his room.

'Ah!' he said, looking up, 'we've settled about Gray. We are going to give him another chance. I think we shall catch him now, and Mr. Brackenbury too.'

'I have not come in about Gray,' said the Junior Dean; 'the fact is, I want you to help me: I'm in a—a horrible fix.'

'Well?' said the senior tutor, 'but he didn't say it encouragingly. 'That woman again!'

'Y-e-s; that — that woman. I'm disappointed in her. I'm dreadfully hurt and—and disappointed.'

'Of course you are!' said the tutor, in the most unfeeling way. 'What else could you expect? I warned you of her.'

'Yes, you warned me. But I never dreamt of—of the misrepresentation that could be made of a simple act of charity. What I have done, I have done from purely philanthropic motives.'

'No doubt,' said the tutor dryly.

'She has heard of my approaching marriage; and she has been to my rooms this morning, and—and——'

'And she has made a row?'

'Yes,' said the Junior Dean with a sigh. 'I'm afraid she is going to give a great deal of trouble. She is in my rooms now.'

The senior tutor whistled.

It is not often a college Don whistles; when such a rare event happens it is portentous.

'Why don't you refuse to see her? Tell Wilkins to turn her out.'

'I—I have asked Wilkins to tell her I am engaged—that I can't see her. And, dear me, I had quite forgotten, I am expecting Miss Gray in my rooms every moment!'

'It would be awkward if they were to meet in your rooms,' said the tutor. 'I'm afraid it would create a scandal. You must do anything to prevent it. I'll go over and tell Wilkins to turn her out. You had better go and stop Miss Gray at the gate: take her into her brother's rooms.'

'I don't think she—Miss De l'Orme—will go quietly if Wilkins attempts to turn her out. I think I had better, perhaps, see her.'

'You had better leave her to Wilkins. You must avoid scandal at any cost—for the sake of the college. It wouldn't do to have a row.'

The senior tutor went out on to the landing;

and then, as if he had remembered something, he came back.

'What did you say the woman's name was?' he asked abruptly.

'De l'Orme. She always called herself Mdlle. Rose De l'Orme. Of course it is her professional name.'

'It was the woman I met coming out of your rooms this morning?'

The Junior Dean nodded assent. He hadn't the heart to speak.

'Rose De l'Orme!' said the senior tutor with a chuckle. 'By Jove! it's little Rosey Pell! Her father was gyp on my staircase. I thought I had seen the face before. I remember her quite well : she used to bring home my washing.'

He went out and shut the door, and left the Junior Dean standing on the hearth-rug. He wasn't looking pained or troubled: he was looking dreadfully ashamed.

The illusion was over; the fond little illusion of Beauty in distress was destroyed in a moment; and he heard the tutor chuckling all the way down the stairs at his folly.

'She used to bring the washing home!' he repeated drearily. And then he began to recall all kinds of incidents of speech and manner that ought to have warned him, if he hadn't been a born idiot, what sort of woman this was.

'She used to bring the washing home!'

And this woman had the assurance to ask him to give up his marriage! She had threatened to force herself upon Molly—to flaunt his gifts in her face—to show her his letters.

Oh, it was too shameful!

He went out hurriedly, with his cheeks burning, and a hard, determined look in his eyes, and his weak lips set quite firm.

He went over to the college gate to inquire if Molly had come in.

The porter was not there, but his deputy was standing at the door of the lodge.

Miss Gray had passed five minutes ago; she had gone in the direction of his rooms. She was with that woman!

Rosey was telling her all her wicked lies—he did not call them misrepresentations now, he called them lies—and there would be a row royal. He set his lips very firm as he went across the court. At the door of his staircase he met the porter coming down the stairs.

'She won't go, sir,' he said, pointing with his thumb in the direction of the Junior Dean's room. 'I've tried everything to get her to go easy, but she won't budge. I think you'll have to see her, sir.'

'I'm going up,' said the Junior Dean; 'but if there's any difficulty, I must ask you, Wilkins, to fetch a policeman.'

The porter opened his eyes to the widest: fetch a policeman for the Queen of Sheba!

Molly was not in the room.

Keith Fellowes gave a sigh of relief; he quite forgot that he hadn't left any instructions about stopping Molly.

'I am sorry you have troubled yourself to call again, Miss De l'Orme,' he said coldly. 'If there is anything you wish to say to me, you can write. I have a pressing engagement just now, and I must ask you to leave the room.'

There was no time for mincing matters. Molly might be here at any moment.

Rosey noted the changed voice, and she looked up at him with a sudden suspicion.

Had he found her out?

His eyes were changed as well as his voice. They were not only cold and stern, but they were indifferent.

All the sympathy and the gentleness, the dulcet, persuasive, pulpit tones, were gone, and his eyes were as unresponsive as fishes'.'

'Well,' said Rosey, 'are you still in the same mind? Are you going on with the marriage, or will you give it up? I don't ask anything more, Mr. Fellowes; I only ask you to give it up.'

'You have no right whatever to interfere in my private affairs. I refuse to discuss them with you. My time is very precious just now, as I have told you; I have an engagement.'

'Then you have decided. You have made up your mind?'

She spoke hoarsely, hurriedly; it was not at all like Rosey's voice.

'That is my concern. It can in no way concern you.'

'We shall see,' she said with a short laugh, that sounded hard and hollow, and there was an unnatural brightness in her eyes. 'I only ask you if you have decided.'

As she was speaking the door opened and

Molly stood in the doorway. She did not knock, and the Junior Dean had not heard her coming up the stairs.

She saw Rosey standing at the table, but her lover was between her and the door.

'Oh!' she said, speaking in her clear, high-pitched voice, 'I didn't know you had anybody with you. I'll come up again presently.'

Before he could stop her she had closed the door, and ran lightly down the stairs.

Rosey looked after her with a strange light in her eyes.

'I don't think I need keep you,' she said hurriedly, with her eyes fixed on the door where Molly had stood. 'If you have decided to—to go on with this marriage, I have nothing more to say. Remember, I have given you a chance! remember, I have warned you!'

She took up her sham muff—she carried it

by the handle now like a bag—and went out of the room.

The Junior Dean heard her go down the stairs, and he dropped into a chair with a white stricken face, and waited for Molly.

Molly was not in sight when Miss De l'Orme reached the quad. She walked slowly back towards the porter's lodge. When half way across the quadrangle, she changed her mind and slipped into a staircase that commanded a view of the Junior Dean's rooms.

As she stood there waiting her eye was arrested by a name painted in white letters over a door—GRAY.

The door was ajar, and she pushed it open. She hadn't any particular motive in opening it; she did it mechanically, with the name in her mind, on her lips.

The room was not empty. Molly was standing beside Jack's writing-table reading his letters. She usually read his letters when she had the opportunity. She was reading a letter he had just received from home, so it was a privileged communication.

She looked up over the top of the letter when Rosey opened the door.

She was perfectly happy, and she looked up with a radiant smile—she thought it was her lover. There was not a single cloud on her horizon, the future was all sunshine, and every pulse of her heart was beating a sweet measure.

In spite of the fog she had been singing all the morning, out of the fulness of her heart of bliss :

'I love the merry, merry sunshine ; it makes my heart so glad !'

It couldn't be gladder ; and at that supreme moment Rosey opened the door, and she saw her over the top of Jack's letter.

She recognised her in a moment as the

lady she had seen in the Junior Dean's room.

'Miss Mary Gray?' said Rosey in her hard voice, and with her eyes glittering.

'Molly,' said the Junior Dean's betrothed sweetly—'Molly Gray.'

Rosey drew her breath hard, and she shut the door.

'I have something to tell you,' she said in a voice that she strove to keep calm, but which shook in spite of her. 'I have a communication to make.'

'Not to me,' said Molly; 'there must be some mistake.'

'There is no mistake if your name is—is Ma—Molly Gray, and if you are about to marry Keith Fellowes.'

'My name is Molly Gray ; and—and I am engaged to marry Mr. Fellowes.'

Molly drew herself up to her full height. She added quite two inches to her stature as she spoke, and her voice was particularly acid. It had lost all its sweetness. She did not like the woman's tone.

Rosey laughed, a hollow mirthless laugh that was quite blood-curdling.

'I don't think you will marry Mr. Fellowes after you have heard what I have to say,' she said scornfully.

Molly flushed scarlet.

'Then I would rather not hear what you have to say,' she said icily.

'I do not ask you whether you would like to hear; you have no alternative : you *must* hear. Keith Fellowes is my lover as well as yours. Keith Fellowes is more to me than ever he will be to you.'

Molly put down Jack's letter on the table, and she walked straight over to the door. 'Will you let me pass?' she said quietly; but she took no other notice of Rosey's words.

Miss De l'Orme put her back against the

door, and a dangerous look came into her eyes, and she put her hand into her muff bag; but she did not take anything out.

'You will not go out of this room until you have heard what I have to say,' said Rosey, with that red light in her eyes that Molly quailed beneath.

'Will you be so good as to say it quickly then?' she said quietly, with a little impatience in her tone. 'I am in a hurry; I have an appointment.'

What could this madwoman have to say to her?

'An appointment you will not keep. I don't think you will want to meet Mr. Fellowes after you have listened to me. Has he ever told you about me? Has he ever told you how he risked his life to save mine? Has he told you of the happy days we spent together at Llanberys? Has he told you of the long walks by the sea-shore in the moonlight, of the solitary rambles in the woods ? Has he told you how he paid my debts, and took lodgings for me in his own name, and has kept me until now ?'

Molly's face had grown crimson while Rosey was speaking, and if the electric spark in her bright eyes could have annihilated anyone, Miss De l'Orme would have been scorched up as she stood.

'When you have quite done, perhaps you will let me go,' she said in her hard metallic voice.

'I have not done yet,' said Rosey. 'You do not believe what I have said. When you see your lover's letters, perhaps you will believe your eyes. See !'

She took a bundle of letters and held them up before Molly's eyes. The writing was quite unmistakable. The Junior Dean wrote as badly as any don could write.

'See ! This was one of the first letters

after he came back to Cambridge'— she tore the letter out of the envelope and spread it open before her.

'" My dear Rose:" he sent me twenty pounds with that letter.' Here is another : " Dear Rose, forgive me for not writing sooner: I send you a little cheque"—that was for twenty-five pounds. Here is his last letter, sent only a fortnight ago. " Dear Rose" again. He sent me fifty pounds then. He took my jewellery out of pawn ; he paid for my dresses ; he paid for the gown I wore last night. He has paid for the clothes I am wearing now.'

Molly looked at the woman with a face that had slowly whitened until it was ashen gray. It had begun to grow pale when her eyes fell on the opening words of the letters her lover had written to this woman. ' Dear Rose '— ' Dear Rose '—the words were burnt into her brain. He had been sending her money with each of those letters. He had only just sent her fifty pounds.

Molly caught at the table to steady herself, and as she stood there the room seemed to go round with her.

The door opened while she was still standing there, looking helplessly at the woman, at her rich dress, at the letters in her hand.

The Junior Dean had opened the door; he had waited in his room for Molly, and as she did not come, he had gone over to her brother's room to look for her. But he did not expect to see Rosey.

He took in the situation at a glance, and he instinctively went over to his betrothed and stood before her.

'Oh, Keith! she murmured, 'is it true?'

'Let him deny it if he can,' said Rosey. 'Ask him if these letters are in his handwriting! Ask him if he sent me fifty pounds the other day!'

Molly turned her eyes upon him with a dumb appeal in them that went to his heart.

'There is gross misrepresentation here,' he said sternly. 'That woman is not to be believed.'

'Oh, Keith! did you send her the money?'

'Yes; I sent her the money.'

His face was very noble, very indignant, and deeply humiliated.

Molly heard no more; she sank down on to a couch that stood near with a little shuddering cry, and put her hands before her face to shut out the sight, and when he bent over her he thought she had fainted.

She had not fainted: she was not made of fainting stuff. She was only shutting out the sight of Rosey, and her rich dress that the Junior Dean had paid for.

'Ask him if he took my things out of pawn; if he paid my debts; if he took lodgings for me in his own name!' said Rosey.

Her voice was choked with passion, and her eyes, that he used to think so soft, were blazing. There was a red light in them he had never seen in any human eyes before. He had seen it, and turned away shuddering from the sight, in the fierce contentions of the lower animals.

'It is quite true,' he said quietly, with an involuntary inflection of scorn in his voice: 'it is quite true that I have done all these things. Have you any other charges to bring against me?'

'I have heard quite enough,' said Molly, rising from the couch with a scarlet spot burning on either cheek, and her head held very erect. 'There is no need to prolong this scene. Pray let me go.'

'Yes,' said the Junior Dean, 'you had better go; and I will deal with this woman.'

'You!' repeated Rosey; but even as she spoke she took something hastily from her bag, and a sudden report was heard in the room.

It was not only heard in the room, but it was heard on the staircase outside, and went echoing round the quadrangle.

Molly heard—felt—the ping of a bullet whizzing past. She was so bewildered that she was not sure for a minute whether anything had happened to herself or not. And then she looked at her lover. He was standing by the table, with a white, strained look on his face, and he was pointing to the door. Molly had no idea that he was shot, but she followed the direction of his pointing hand—it was his left hand—and she saw the woman hurriedly leaving the room.

And even as she looked the outstretched hand dropped by his side and he staggered to the couch she had just risen from.

In a moment the room was full of men, and they were gathering round him.

'What is it?' 'Is anybody shot?' 'What has happened?'

There was no one to give any answer, for the Junior Dean had fainted.

# CHAPTER XXVIII.

### A CAMBRIDGE SCANDAL.

There never had been such a scandal in Cambridge. The papers were full of it. There were the most conflicting rumours afloat ; and every one was false.

It was the chief topic of conversation in every college common room. It was spoken of in whispers in chapel ; it was talked about freely in Hall.

Rumour had a busy time of it. She picked up all the tittle-tattle she could find—and she found a good deal—and she pieced it together, and she made a very pretty story.

In the first place she circulated a report

that the Junior Dean was dead—killed by the hand of a Mrs. Junior Dean—and that that unhappy lady, maddened by her wrongs, had committed the deed in a moment of frenzy, and had afterwards put an end to her own existence.

But this report was entirely without foundation. The Junior Dean was not dead. He was wounded in the shoulder, and his right arm was disabled. He had run a very near chance of his life. If the course of the bullet had slightly deviated Rumour would not have lied.

He was in a critical condition for several hours; and while he lay unconscious Rosey was lodged in prison.

Nobody had seen her leave the college, and if it hadn't been for the senior tutor's recollection of the old time when she used to bring home his washing, she would not have been recognised. Keith Fellowes was too ill to attend when Rosey was charged at the police court with letting off a revolver with intent to murder, and she was remanded for several days to enable him to appear. It was quite as well that he was shut up in that darkened room, and saw no one but the nurse and the doctor, during those dark December days.

Oh, if he had only known!

But luckily he didn't know. He didn't even know that Rosey was in prison. He had fondly hoped that she had escaped—and that a scandal had been avoided.

He didn't know that she was posing as a victim—an injured woman maddened by her wrongs.

He didn't know that the sympathy of the 'Varsity, of the town, of the whole country, indeed, was with her; that a fund had been started for her defence; that she was cheered when she appeared in court; that a great crowd had followed her back to the prison with a noisy demonstration of sympathy and approval.

He didn't know that his name was in everyone's mouth ; that it was hooted in every college quad ; that it was reviled in the public print ; and that he had been burnt in effigy in the market-place.

Happily he knew none of these things.

He didn't even see his letters. He asked for them once or twice, but they were not forthcoming. They would keep very well, the doctor told him—and they kept.

There was a letter from Molly among them, and one in a big sprawly hand, with the postmark of a little village in Devonshire ; and one in a woman's angular writing that was not unfamiliar to him, but it did not smell nicely this time.

Fever had supervened on the wound, and perfect quiet had been ordered, so it was quite as well that he did not see his letters.

Molly had written her letter to her lover when she had gone back to Newnham, but she had made no further sign.

She showed no external signs of wanting sympathy or condolence. She did her work with her wonted untidiness and irregularity, with a smile on her lips and an unclouded brow. She took her seat at all the college meals—the students of Newnham take their food together ; they do not breakfast, like the men, in the seclusion of their own rooms—her seat at Hall was never once vacant, and she had an excellent appetite. Indeed, this rupture with her lover had no other external effect than to make her hungry. She never talked about the scandal that was on everybody's tongue. She refused to discuss the subject with anyone.

Adela was most anxious to hear all about it, but she had to be content with the scanty information afforded by the newspapers, and they made no mention of Molly.

No one would have guessed that anything had happened to mar the happiness of her life. She showed no outward sign or token; she did not even weep in secret.

Only those who were most observant, or who loved her best, discovered that her cheek was flushed more than usual, and her eyes a little too bright.

Dorothy Piggott discovered this as Molly hung over her. Her own heart was fluttering with its new-found happiness, and it had an instinctive sympathy with *affaires des cœurs*. She put her arms around her, and laid her cheek against hers, and murmured some tender words of condolence.

'It is all over, Dolly,' said Molly in her hard voice, and with an attempt to be sprightly. 'The house will have to be given up, and the furniture sent back — it isn't even paid for—and oh! dear, I don't know what can be done about the new kitchen range. I suppose I shall have to bring it here.'

It was no use Molly pretending; Dorothy Piggott's eyes were not so dull as they looked: they were not full of mathematics now, they were soft and tender; love had lifted the veil, and she saw through Molly's little feeble pretence.

'I wouldn't bring it here yet,' she said softly, with her arm still round Molly's neck, and her cheek against hers; 'I would wait until—until—this has blown over, and Mr. Fellowes has had an opportunity to explain. Remember, he is in bed now, weak and helpless; when he is able he will explain. I am sure he will explain.'

'He has explained already,' said Molly bitterly. 'He has acknowledged that the very clothes that wretched woman wore he paid for. Oh! you should have seen her dress. Such a sealskin jacket and muff!'—

here Molly shuddered—'and a gown trailing on the floor ; and *it was lined with silk!* I heard the rustle of it when the woman came into the room ; and I in an old serge gown, and a jacket I have worn for years! Oh, it was shameful!'

'You do not know all. I am sure he will be able to explain. Can't you trust him, Molly?'

'Trust him!' repeated Molly scornfully— she really had a very unpleasant voice ; 'trust him, when he acknowledges to my face that he has been keeping this woman for months— that he has paid her debts—that he has been sending her money continually—that he has written her letters in the tenderest language : she showed me heaps of them!'

'Did you read them?'

'Read them? No, I did not read them. I saw the heading—there could be no mistake about it, in his own writing—" Dear Rose,"

"My dear Rose!" Faugh! it makes me sick!'

Molly would have had reason to be sick if she had seen a letter which Jack picked up on the floor of his room after Rosey had gone.

When she had gathered up her papers so hurriedly, one had escaped her and fallen on the floor, and there Jack had found it hours after.

He read it with a lowering brow, and he took it over to Mr. Gray, the tutor of Clare, and showed it to him. And Mr. Gray wrote to his brother at the little Rectory in Devonshire, and gave him the particulars of the case; and he had further told him that the chief evidence against his daughter's lover was not from the lips of the abandoned woman who had wounded him, but from his own hand. That, in fact, a document in his possession, in the handwriting of Keith

Fellowes, fully proved that he had been in the habit of sending this woman money.

The Rector did not ask to see the document in question. He had read the account of the fray in the newspapers before he received his brother's letter, and he had drawn his own conclusions.

A great many people drew their own conclusions from the newspaper version of the story. All were premature; and the majority were unfair.

The view that Molly's father took of the case was not only premature and unfair, but it was prejudiced.

He had always regarded with distrust a suitor who could not find time to run down and ask his permission in person—it was not the way things were managed in his days—but took himself off through all the long vacation to a remote watering-place, on the pretence of earning a paltry fifty pounds, when he was squandering hundreds all the time upon an actress.

In this frame of mind he wrote to the Junior Dean and broke off the match, so it was quite as well that the nurse obeyed the doctor's instructions, not to give him his letters.

Yet the letter that Jack picked up under his table was not in itself conclusive of the Junior Dean's guilt. It was only when taken in conjunction with other circumstances that it made his conduct look culpable.

It was a very short letter, evidently written in haste; and it was written on the college note-paper. There was no attempt whatever at concealment; it was written with the most unblushing effrontery:

' My dear Rose' (it began),
'I send you a cheque for thirty pounds. I am writing in haste to catch this

post, that you may have the money by return.

'The chapel-bell is ringing, and I have no time for more.

'Yours,
'Keith Fellowes.'

An expert, holding it up to the light, would have observed that there was a certain thinness of the paper, and a disturbance of the surface, after the word 'Yours,' that indicated that an erasure had been made: there was still the tail of a *y* faintly visible, preceded by an *l*, if anyone had looked for it, as if the letter had not originally terminated with that endearing word 'Yours,' that meant so many things.

But Jack was not an expert, and the erasure had been very cleverly managed. It might have stood originally 'truly,' 'sincerely,' 'faithfully,' or any other purely conventional,

unmeaning expression. It stood, however,
' Yours.'

So Jack read it, and the tutor of Clare
read it, and Mrs. Gray read it, and shook her
head at it, and sighed : whatever should she
do with those kitchen things ? And Adela
read it, and grew furiously red over it, and
went back to Newnham and told Molly all
about it.

Perhaps that was the bitterest drop of gall
in Molly's cup ; it was like a knife in a new
wound.

' Oh !' said Molly coolly, though her heart
was hot within her ; ' how very kind of you to
come and tell me ! I knew it all before,
dear ; she showed me the letter ; I know all
about the " dear Roses " and the cheques—I
have seen all the letters.'

And she swept out of the room with her
head erect, and quite an unusual amount of
dignity ; and Adela did not see that her lips

were trembling, nor that when she had got into the corridor she ran upstairs to her own room, and shut and bolted the door, and flung herself down beside her bed, and buried her face in a cushion that no one should hear the cry she could not keep back :

'Oh, Keith ! Keith !'

It was on this very day, the eve of Rosey's second examination, that there was an *auto da fé* in the market-place.

The Cambridge market-place is not a covered, enclosed space. It has no covering whatever, and, except on market days, it is only a vast paved square lying at the back of the 'Varsity Church, and fronting the Guildhall.

It was not market day, and the few stalls that had been standing during the day for the sale of vegetables and flowers were all cleared away. It was past ten o'clock when a little crowd of gownsmen began to collect in the dark, deserted square. The crowd grew rapidly, for the Union had just opened its doors and poured out a full house; and all, with one accord, made their way to the market-place.

A thin line of blue smoke rose slowly up from a dark pile, which nobody had seen before, and which seemed to have sprung out of the ground, and presently a flame shot up into the air as high as the market-cross.

It lighted up the houses round, and the Guildhall, and the tower and pinnacles of Great St. Mary's. It shot up so fierce and sudden a volume of flame that it seemed, for a moment, as if the whole town was on fire.

As the flames shot up there was a dull roar from the crowd, and the men on the outer edge pressed forward to get a better view of what was going on in front.

A wide circle was cleared round the fire, and in the lurid glare two black figures were slowly carrying between them a limp effigy, that looked very much like a college don. It was habited in a long Master of Arts gown that dragged on the ground behind it; and it was so weak in the back that it had to be supported on both sides. A storm of shouting and hissing arose from the crowd as it was slowly perambulated round the funeral pile; and when, at a given signal, it was hurled into the midst of the fire, a terrific howl arose that might have been heard all over Cambridge.

The Proctors heard it, and hurried to the scene of action. They were, unfortunately, at the other end of the town, waiting at the theatre door for the undergraduates to come out; and as one of them happened to be fat, and the other happened to be lame, it took them a long time to reach it.

Of whatever materials the obnoxious don was composed, he burnt well.

The flames from the funeral pile shot up

with renewed vigour, and St. Mary's Church glowed red in the lurid light, as if the venerable building were itself in flames ; and the howling and hooting that were going on around it were enough to awaken the quiet dead who slept beneath its stones.

It brought the townspeople in troops out of their houses ; and the mob thickened, and the din increased, and when the object of the *auto da fé* became known, the hooting and the execrations increased tenfold.

When the Proctors arrived on the scene, they had to break through a cordon of townspeople, before they reached the inner circle of gownsmen, and then, and only then, did they discover, 'mid a shower of sparks and a huge volume of smoke, that Rosey's friends were burning the Junior Dean.

They caught a few men, and the bull-dogs took notes of a great many others.

Among the men captured was Jack, who

was caught red-handed introducing a bundle of fire-lighters beneath the half-consumed effigy of what had once been his future brother-in-law.

## CHAPTER XXIX.

### RUSTICATED.

WHILE Jack was disporting himself in the market-place, Mr. Flynt was occupied with his little stratagem in the court outside St. Stephen's College.

It happened to be the court into which Jack's window looked. A great many windows looked out into the court, and the men inside them, behind the bars, looked out like caged animals, or prisoners charged with some serious crime. It was a very doleful court, and the barred windows, and the men looking out from the gratings, didn't at all look to belong to the nineteenth century.

The senior tutor chose a particular window for the scene of his operations, and there, under the cover of the night, he set his little trap. It was a very harmless little trap, and he set it with a reel of black cotton and a few pins.

When he had set the trap to his satisfaction he went back to his rooms.

He didn't go straight to his rooms; he called in on his way to see the Junior Dean, who was sitting up for the first time after his accident.

He wasn't fully dressed even now; he wore a dressing-gown, and had his arm in a sling. There was a white change in his face, as of a man who has passed through a severe mental struggle, and he looked weak and despondent.

He was nibbling a biscuit, and by his side, wearing an air of modest conviviality, was a glass of toast-and-water.

He looked up with a feeble smile when the senior tutor entered, and motioned him to take a seat on the other side of the fireplace. He had nothing in the way of refreshment to offer him but toast-and-water.

'You are not looking so well to-night, Fellowes,' said the tutor, taking his seat opposite to him; 'you are looking tired and worn.'

'Yes,' said the Junior Dean with a sigh, 'I am very tired. I have been reading my letters.'

He did not say that there was a letter from Molly releasing him from his engagement, and another from her father declining in the most emphatic terms the honour he proposed to do him in becoming his son-in-law.

'There is a letter from—from her here,' selecting a letter from the heap by his side; 'I ought to have had it a week ago.'

Mr. Flynt took up the letter cautiously, as

if there were infection in it, and read it a long way off. It began abruptly—an untidy scrawl, blurred and blotted as if with tears :

'Forgive me,' it began. 'Oh, how can you forgive me? I did not intend to injure *you*. Heaven is my witness that the shot was not intended for you. On my knees I implore your forgiveness, and I swear before Heaven I will never, never trouble you again !

'This once—only this once—I beg, I implore, your forgiveness. Some words of yours are ringing in my ears now; I heard them one summer's night at Llanberys, and the sound of the sea came in at the open church door and mingled its voice with yours. I hear it now with the solemn echo of the waves:

'" If thy brother sin against thee seven times in one day, and seven times in the day turn to thee saying, I repent, thou shalt forgive him."

'I have sinned but this once, and I come to you on my knees saying : I repent. Can you forgive me ?

'ROSEY.'

Mr. Flynt read it through with a frown gathering on his brow, and threw it down impatiently.

'What will you do?' he said.

'Do? I can do but one thing after that letter. I shall withdraw the charge. I shall not appear against her.'

'Fellowes, are you mad ?' gasped the senior tutor. 'You don't know what you are saying. For the sake of the college, for the honour of the University, you are bound to prosecute this woman.'

The Junior Dean flushed faintly.

'It is my own private concern,' he said. 'I did not make any charge against her. I do not make any now. It has nothing to do with the University.'

'It has a great deal to do with the University. You don't know—how should you, lying shut up here all this time?—the stir this scandal has made. It is on everybody's tongue. It has been grossly misrepresented; it has been exaggerated almost past recognition; it is calculated to do a great deal of mischief to the college—to the University, in fact.'

The Junior Dean covered his eyes with his hand, as if to shut out the light. It had grown thin and white during this week, and Mr. Flynt saw that it trembled as he held it before his eyes.

'I am sorry,' he said presently, 'I am very sorry; but I cannot alter my decision. It is my own affair, it is not the business of the college; I shall not, after that letter, prosecute the unhappy woman.'

'I am sure you are wrong,' said the senior tutor impatiently. 'If you only knew what people are saying about you outside, you would go through with this case, if only to vindicate your character.'

' My character ?' he repeated, with a little wan smile—he was thinking of that letter from Molly's father—' it is too late to think about that now. People, as you say, have already settled that point. No ; I have quite made up my mind not to prosecute : no personal considerations should induce me to alter it.'

And even as he spoke a noise arose without ; a trampling of footsteps on the stones beneath, and a hooting and yelling of many voices under the window.

The tutor drew aside the blind and looked out into the quadrangle. It may be that the men beneath recognised the familiar figure, for the voices were suddenly hushed, and the men beat a precipitate retreat. But in the sky, above the battlements of the college, he caught a glimpse of red flame, and a shower of sparks rose up behind the intervening buildings, and it dawned upon him that something unusual was going on in the market-place.

'What is it?' the Junior Dean asked; 'what are the men doing?' He could see from his seat by the fire the dull red glow in the sky; and he couldn't help hearing the shouting in the streets outside and in the quad beneath.

'The friends of—of "the unhappy woman," as you are pleased to call her, are making a demonstration. Now you can see the view that the world—not the world only, but every undergraduate in Cambridge—takes of the case. Now you can understand why it is desirable, for the sake of the University, to press the charge, and have the matter thoroughly sifted.'

A terrific howl came from without as he

spoke, from the direction of the chapel, and with it a crash of broken glass.

'Good heavens!' exclaimed the tutor, 'they are breaking the windows of the chapel. I should think you would alter your mind now!' he said grimly, as he hurried out of the room; and the Junior Dean heard him presently tearing across the quad in the direction of the chapel.

When it became known the next morning that the Junior Dean had refused to prosecute the woman who had fired at him, the indignation of the University knew no bounds.

If any proof of his guilt were wanting, surely it was here. Nothing could be more conclusive. He was afraid of the revelations that would follow if the woman were examined in court, and he had every motive for hushing the case up.

This was the opinion of everyone in Cambridge, and it was shared by his friends in the University.

Perhaps no one was more surprised at the withdrawal of the charge than the prisoner. She looked deathly pale when placed in the dock, and was so weak that she could not stand without support. The week's confinement seemed to have told upon her. There was a white, cold, dead look on her face as of one stricken to the heart; and her figure seemed to have lost all its roundness and subtle grace of movement. The *frou-frou* whisper of her skirts was silent.

The men who had seen her in her beauty, in that trailing apricot gown, at the concert at the Guildhall, could hardly recognise her now. With the instinctive chivalry of youth, that ever sides with the weak, every man among them had become her particular knight-errant, and espoused her cause.

There was an uproar in the court, and a

scene of hooting and confusion ensued when it became known that the Junior Dean of St. Stephen's had withdrawn the charge.

Even Rosey's white, dead face flushed rosy red, and the colour came back to her lips. The place, with its sea of faces, swam round her, and she would have fallen if a warder had not placed her in a chair.

There was nothing to be done but to discharge the prisoner. The magistrate did his part with a very bad grace; and everybody went away grumbling and disappointed.

What revelations had they been cheated of!

A great washing-day of soiled linen was expected; and, lo! there was no linen to wash.

Rosey was cheered tremendously on leaving the court, and some of her admirers followed the fly back to the little house in the Newmarket Road.

There was a meeting of the Dons of St.

Stephen's after chapel, and men who saw them crossing the court remarked that they looked very grave.

They had reason to look grave : one of the chapel-windows was broken. St. Stephen's was justly proud of its old stained-glass windows—some of them dated from the fifteenth century; and people interested in such things came from a distance to see them. It was one of these old windows that was broken; the loss was quite irreparable.

No wonder the Dons looked grave; the court had been so full of men the previous night that it was impossible to pick out the offenders. A notice was posted up requesting the men who were creating a disturbance in the court on the previous evening to send in their names to the senior tutor.

Not any names were sent in. Probably the men did not recognise that a little harmless shouting was creating a disturbance.

After chapel the Dean called attention to the outrage that had been committed—he nearly shed tears in doing it—and requested the malefactors to send in their names before Hall.

The men went into Hall a trifle graver than usual, for everybody felt that something serious was impending. But nobody availed themselves of the Dean's invitation.

After Hall an awful rumour went round the courts that, unless the real malefactor came forward, all the men who were in college at the time would be 'sent down.'

Mr. Brackenbury was crossing the quadrangle when some men came up to him with stricken faces and told him the awful news.

'I hope they'll like it,' he said with a laugh ; ' I'm sure I shall be very glad to go down.'

' There are a great many that won't,' said another man ruefully ; ' it's infernally hard on other fellows to suffer for a cad that hasn't the common honesty to come forward!' and he turned on his heels and went back to his rooms with a look of something very like scorn in his eyes.

Mr. Brackenbury smiled pleasantly and went over to Jack's rooms.

'Have you heard what's up?' said Jack moodily.

'Yes—a general exodus.'

'You don't mean to say, Brackenbury——' interrupted Jack, and a dusky red colour crept up under his skin, and his eyes were very bright under his heavy brows.

'I don't mean to say anything,' said the other coolly, 'if that's what you mean. If the rest go down, I suppose I shall go down with them;' and he hummed a delightful little tune.

Jack rapped out some interjections that are not to be found in Lindley Murray, while Mr.

Brackenbury smoked his pipe with imperturbable good-humour.

'When you have quite finished, old man,' he said sweetly, 'we'll go and see how the fair Rosey has borne her long confinement.'

He went out; and Jack, when he had quite recovered from his ill-humour, went out too.

The porter at the door saw him go out; but he did not see him come in again.

He was not in his rooms at eleven o'clock when the senior tutor happened to look in. At twelve he had not entered by the college-gate, and his room was still untenanted.

In the small hours of the morning, two men in academicals turned down a lane that skirted the college buildings, a dark, unfrequented lane that swallowed them up in its shadow. Half-way down the lane one of the men disappeared, while the other stood coolly shaking out the ashes of his pipe in the lane.

He had not disappeared very far. He had

only made a leap up to one of the windows, and was hanging on by the bars. He had evidently hung on by that particular bar before. He passed his hand between the bars, and the whole grating presently swung back like a door, and left the window free.

The window opened with a touch, and Jack sprang lightly into the room. At least, he didn't spring very lightly, for he was intercepted midway, and fell heavily into the arms of the senior tutor.

'What the deuce——' Jack began.

'Ah! now I've caught you,' said the tutor when he had recovered his breath; and after that there was little more to be said.

Mr. Brackenbury, knocking the ashes out of his pipe in the lane below, heard the scuffle going on in the room above. He also heard the well-known voice of Mr. Flynt. He could not possibly mistake it.

He tranquilly retraced his steps, and, after

a sufficient time had elapsed, presented himself at his college gate.

The next morning Jack was among the first arrivals at chapel. It was his first attendance at morning chapel this term, and men looked across the benches at him during the service with a strange question in their eyes.

Jack saw it there, and he knew exactly what it meant. His face was grave and resolved—and it was also ashamed.

He could not meet the silent reproof in the eyes of the grim, not unkindly old tutors, who had for nearly three years been trying to save him from himself, to keep him straight.

He saw it all now, as he sat in the dim light of his college chapel for the last time. His heart was hot within him, and some feeling of shame brought a strange mist before his eyes. Oh, if he could only live those three years over again!

He thrust the shame back, and put a cool face upon it, and walked out of chapel behind the Dons with an air of unconcern, though he knew he had left for ever his old life behind him.

No more, henceforth, would those old familiar stones re-echo to his tread. The old, old Dons who slept in the darkness and the dust beneath his feet were not more dead to them than he would henceforth be.

He had a furious headache, though he had gone to chapel in spite of it, and he had no appetite for his breakfast.

The men were standing about in groups in the quadrangle as he came out of chapel, and there were mutterings of discontent heard everywhere. The rumour of the previous night had been confirmed. If the men who committed the outrage, and broke the old glass in the chapel windows did not come forward, all the men who were in college at the time were to be sent down.

'It's a beastly shame!' he overheard a man saying as he passed. 'I was in my room reading, with my door sported, and I'm sent down. I shall lose the term, and have to come up again after the Tripos. It's six months out of my life—the best six months. Oh, it's too bad!'

Little Blantyre came across the quad beside him. His face was almost as white as his surplice. 'Oh,' he said, 'can it be true, Gray? Are we really to be sent down?'

'I'm afraid so,' said Jack gloomily.

'I—I was in my room, with my oak sported—in fact, I was in bed—when it happened.'

He blushed furiously when he made this admission. He had only left school a few months; and he had just begun to learn that it was not good form to go to bed early, or to keep out of a row, if you could possibly get into one. It showed blood; therefore he blushed.

'The truth was, Gray,' he went on humbly, with that tell-tale colour in his face—'I don't mind telling you—I was in the crowd that night in the market-place. At least, I was on the edge of the crowd. I should awfully have liked to have been in the middle of it. I should have liked to have brought over all my fire-lighters and added to the blaze. I should have liked to have hooted and yelled with the rest; but—I hope you won't think it cowardly, Gray—I went straight back to my rooms and sported my oak—and went to bed. I had to stuff my fingers in my ears all the way back to the college to keep out the noise of the fellows shouting. If I had heard them I should have gone back. It was only the thought of my mother, and how it would disappoint her if I lost my scholarship, that made me run away. I hope it wasn't cowardly, Gray.'

The young scholar was inside the door, with his cap in his hand, waiting anxiously for Jack's verdict. Somehow, Jack was his hero.

Jack closed the door behind him, and laid his hand kindly on the lad's shoulder.

'My dear fellow,' he said, and his voice was a trifle husky as he spoke, 'it was about the manliest thing that I've heard of. It was certainly the bravest thing done on that wretched night. The game wasn't worth the candle. The game never *is* worth the candle. I've come to the conclusion—and if I had my time to go over again I should do it myself— that there are times when the manly thing to do is—to run away.'

Jack sat down to his lonely breakfast; the little scholar had gone back to his rooms. He had not sat down five minutes before a message was brought to him that the Dean would like to speak to him in his rooms at ten o'clock.

He knew exactly what that message meant. He was what, in figurative undergraduate language, is termed ' hauled.'

He saw Mr. Flynt crossing the quad before him in the direction of the Dean's rooms, and the Master was coming across from the Lodge.

His heart ought to have thumped at these premonitory signs ; but in point of fact it refused to thump.

He met Mr. Brackenbury crossing the quad in a very magnificent smoking-cap that one of his feminine adorers had recently sent him ; he was going to breakfast in it to another man's rooms, and he nodded gaily to Gray as he saw him enter the Dean's staircase, and made a playful motion with his thumb towards the college gateway, suggestive of being sent down.

Jack didn't return his nod, and there was a fierce gleam in his eyes, beneath his heavy brows, as he climbed up the Dean's staircase.

The Master of Stephen's, and the senior tutor, and the Dean were waiting to receive him, and he ought to have been horribly agitated, and had a dreadful thumping at his heart.

That encounter with Mr. Brackenbury in the quad had acted as an alterative, or a sedative rather, and he was quite calm and collected when he came into the room.

It was a *mauvais quart d'heure*—it lasted quite a quarter of an hour ; but Jack remained cool through it all. He answered all the questions that were put to him without the slightest reserve. The game was up, there were no terms to be made, and it was quite as well to make an honourable capitulation. At least, there was one point on which he was reserved : he refused to give the names of any other men who had used that mode of ingress and egress.

He acknowledged to having used it since his freshman's year. He did not say that it was at the instigation of another man that little arrangement of the bars had been made. He did not say that he had been persuaded to allow his window to be tampered with for another man's convenience, and that for a whole term he had himself refused to use it. He did not say that another man had instructed the locksmith, whose ingenuity had contrived it (he had also been so obliging, in order to excuse the locksmith's visit, as to break the lock of his room).

He did not acknowledge that he had been made a cat's-paw of.

He stood up looking very pale and grave, and almost noble, and took the whole credit to himself.

And then, when he was sent down for a year, he came back into the room where the Dons were assembled, as if he had forgotten something, and had just remembered it.

'About the glass in the chapel,' he said: 'I am very sorry to have done such wanton mischief. It was I who threw the stone. It was I only who did it.'

He was dreadfully pale; but his face was quite calm, and he was perfectly self-possessed.

'You?' said the Dean—he didn't believe him—'surely not you, Gray?'

'Yes, sir. It was I who threw it. Who else should? It was my sister.'

And then he flushed scarlet—he didn't mean to bring Molly's name into it.

It was an awful offence, and he had given a reason for committing it—an unworthy reason.

There was but one course open to the Dons. The college property had been wantonly destroyed; a quite irretrievable loss had been sustained.

Jack was rusticated.

# CHAPTER XXX.

### JACK GOES DOWN.

It was all over the college in no time. The news spread like wild-fire through every court, up every staircase.

There wasn't a man in the college that didn't know that Jack was rusticated. Not sent down to come up in a year or two, but rusticated.

It was with a spasm of relief that men heard that that awful fiat had been revoked; that the college would not go down in a body; that they might still keep their term.

Some compassion was felt for the luckless undergraduate—the Curtius Mettius of St.

Stephen's—who had propitiated the vengeance of the Dons by the sacrifice of himself.

The men were coming and going all the morning to wish Jack good-bye, and to tell him how awfully sorry they were that he was sent down. It dreadfully interfered with his packing, and it was not at all a cheerful thing, when it really came to it, this saying 'good-bye.'

Something choked in his throat more than once during that memorable morning. He couldn't help thinking, as he saw the men hurrying across the court to a lecture, how the old life, the chapels, the lectures, the halls, the wines, and all the fun on the river and in the football fields, would go on just the same without him.

Little Blantyre came in after the lecture, and found Jack in the midst of his packing. At least, he had turned everything out of his drawers on the floor, but he hadn't got anything into his bags. He had spent all the morning over packing his books.

The door of the inner room was open, and Jack was standing in the midst of his *lares*— a picture of despondency and gloom. His linen was scattered about all over the floor, and his dress suit and his flannels were lying in a heap under his bed.

He didn't know where to begin.

'I'm so sorry, Gray,' said the tender-hearted little fellow, wringing his hand, and looking very much as if he were going to cry. 'I'm awfully sorry ! I shall remember you all my life as the best fellow I ever met. I hope you won't forget me, Gray.'

Jack smiled. Nobody else had asked him to remember them, and this boy hadn't been up three months.

'Yes,' he said, rather huskily, 'I'm not likely to forget you, Blantyre. I'm not likely to forget that lesson of true manliness—of self-restraint—you gave me this morning. If I had learnt it earlier, I should not be going down now ;' and he made a dash at a portmanteau and applied himself vigorously to his packing.

'I should like you to have something to remember me by, Gray,' he said.

The little fox terrier that he had smuggled into the college had followed him into the room, and stood watching, with a puzzled expression on his face and one shiny black ear cocked on one side, the preparations that were going on. Blantyre took him up and stroked him softly—a long, lingering stroke, and put him into Jack's arms.

'I want you to have Peter,' he said, in rather a shaky voice. 'He likes you as well as he likes me ; and I'm sure you'll be a kind master to him. You don't know when you are in trouble what a comfort it is to have a little dog. You needn't tell him anything ;

he understands all about it See how he's licking your hand now !'

That foolish Jack was quite cut up. The tears had started to his eyes, and he had the greatest difficulty to keep them from falling on Peter's back. The boy's sympathy, and the dog's, had touched him, in spite of himself.

'No, Blantyre; thank you all the same, I wouldn't take Peter—dear old Peter' (and he was foolish enough to kiss the top of the dog's nose, or else the dog kissed him— perhaps it was mutual) 'away from you for the world. I can remember you very well without Peter;' and again he plunged into the packing.

'It isn't taking him away from me; I'm not going to bring him up next term. I can't keep him in college without breaking the rules, and I'm not going to run any more risks. If you won't have him, I shall have to give him away to someone else.'

But Jack was not to be persuaded.

When his packing was finished, he put on his big overcoat and an ugly hard hat. He had left, hanging up behind his door, his ragged gown and his limp, disreputable cap; he would never—never more have occasion to wear them again. He was no longer a member of the University. He had tasted that bitterest of all forms of dismissal—the Boot.

He put on the everyday clothes of society, and, taking a friendly stick, walked briskly in the direction of Newnham.

Molly was expectant, and alone. She had been expectant all the morning. She had not heard the result of the examination at the Guildhall on the previous day, and she was too proud to inquire, and everyone hesitated to tell her.

She sat nervous and expectant in her room; she jumped at the sound of a knock at her door. And when the servant told her that a gentleman was waiting for her in the hall, she trembled all over. She thought it was her lover.

She went out into the passage that struck quite a chill into her—that bitter north-west passage—and her heart began to thump dreadfully.

It was only Jack, and he had come to say good-bye.

She saw at the first glance that something was amiss. It was not the old Jack. His eyes were graver, and his look was steadier. The old boyish look—the youthfulness and the fun—had gone out of it.

'I have come to say good-bye, Molly,' he said, in a voice that seemed new and strange to her; 'I am going home. I have been sent down. Poor old pater! I'm awfully sorry for him. It'll be hard on him.'

His eyes were shining, and in the dim light

Molly did not notice that he passed his sleeve across his eyes.

'Sent down! Whatever have you done, Jack?' she gasped. Molly was so full of her own trouble, that she could hardly comprehend a misfortune happening to another.

'I have done enough to be sent down,' said Jack gloomily; 'but I didn't come here to talk to you about that. I came here to speak about—about a girl—a friend of yours—a Miss Piggott. She seems a good sort of a girl, and—I'm very sorry for her—she is being fooled by a scoundrel——'

'Do you mean Mr. Brackenbury?' interrupted Molly, turning very white.

'Yes,' muttered Jack hoarsely; 'if it is not gone too far, if you have any influence with her, save her from this folly. You—you have known what it is to be deceived—save her from this unprincipled scoundrel! Warn her, while there is yet time, that he is as false as hell !'

Jack went away and left Molly standing in the hall white and trembling.

Adela found her there ; she had heard that Jack had called, and she had come reluctantly away from her work. She saw the startled look in Molly's eyes, and she guessed in a moment the purport of her brother's visit.

'So Jack has been to tell you the result of the trial,' she said sweetly. 'I wonder you had not heard it before.'

'I have not heard now,' said Molly.

'Not that Mr. Fellowes has refused to prosecute—that he has tacitly admitted the woman's claims, and let her go free? I thought everybody in Cambridge had heard it. Why, they burnt his effigy in the marketplace, and the men of his college broke the chapel-windows——'

She was speaking to unheeding ears, for

Molly had vanished down the chill Arctic passage.

Jack went back to St. Stephen's; he had no other good-byes to make. He had not a parting word to say to anyone in Cambridge; but he had a few words with Mr. Brackenbury before he went away. He saw him crossing the quadrangle in the direction of his staircase as he came through the college gate, and he went up after him.

Mr. Brackenbury had not been one of the men of St. Stephen's who had come over to Jack's rooms, after it was known that he was going down, to express his regret. He had gone in and out of the court two or three times during the morning, but he had passed on the other side.

He had got on that magnificent smoking-cap when Jack entered his room, and he was smoking a short black pipe.

'Come in!' he shouted in the most affable

way when Jack banged at his door; but he didn't look particularly delighted to see him.

'I've come about that bill,' Jack began abruptly.

'Yes,' said Mr. Brackenbury, with his dreamy smile, as if recalling it by an effort of memory. 'Yes, to be sure—that little bill. There is no need to remember it yet. There are two or three months to remember it in.'

'Six weeks,' said Jack moodily. 'You remember you promised me to make it right by that time. You were going to sell some confounded picture.'

'Respect my feelings, Jack. A portrait of my grandmother, by Romney. I've sent the old woman to Christie's, but heaven only knows when she's coming off. However, I'll see Beelzebub about the bill, and make it square. I hear she's going to fetch a neat thousand. Think of the old woman being good for that! Her grandchildren will have reason to rise up and call her blessed!'

Mr. Brackenbury laughed a delightful little low laugh that might almost be termed a chuckle, and Jack, with his moody brows and his empty pockets, turned away in disgust.

'By the way, Brackenbury,' he said, coming back to the table where Mr. Brackenbury was brewing some kind of 'cup' with the assistance of a spirit-bottle and the kettle, ' can you let me have the couple of sovereigns I lent you last night at Pell's? I want them for my journey home; I'm quite cleaned out.'

Mr. Brackenbury considered a moment.

' Yes,' he said musingly, 'I really think I can. It is not often that I am able to repay a loan so quickly. Like you, I was cleaned out yesterday; but a good angel came to my aid, and I had a run of luck last night.'

Mr. Brackenbury took from his pocket as he spoke a roll of crisp notes that sent quite a low whisper thrilling through the room as he passed his hand tenderly over them.

Smiler was looking in at the window, and he gave a plaintive 'Miaow!' to be let in. He thought it was something to eat.

Mr. Brackenbury selected a fair virgin bank-note—they were all fresh virgin notes—and threw it across the table to Jack.

'This is for five,' said Jack, taking it up, with a faint colour coming in his face, 'and I only lent you two.'

'Oh, there were two or three sovs. I borrowed the other night——'

'Five,' interrupted Jack moodily.

'Oh, was it five? then put the difference against them.'

Jack stuffed the note in his waistcoat pocket, and said good-bye, but he didn't offer to shake hands.

'I am sorry you are going down, Jack,' said Mr. Brackenbury, as he was going away.

'You should learn to keep a still tongue. That unruly member of yours will get you into trouble yet.'

Jack rapped out a very naughty word. It is to be hoped that there was no recording angel in Mr. Brackenbury's room. Smiler was looking in at his window, with his back up, and his eyes glowing like balls of fire in the darkness. Jack ever after associated this last interview—this last meeting he ever had in the flesh—with the Mephistopheles who had ruined his University career, with the distorted outline of the black cat on the leads, and the glowing eyeballs at the window.

'Good-bye, Brackenbury,' he called out when he was half-way down the stairs. 'You'll be sure to remember that bill?'

'All right, old man; I give you my word upon it.'

'You won't forget, now; six weeks, remember! You promise me to remember?'

'Promise? I'll take my oath, if you like.'

For the last time in his life Jack heard Mr. Brackenbury's pleasant little laugh; and he heard him at the same time open the window to admit Smiler, and the thud of the creature leaping to the floor.

This was the last sound he heard at St. Stephen's.

When he reached the railway-station, the train was already at the platform. He jumped into an empty carriage, and was wrapping himself in his rugs, when somebody opened the door. It was little Blantyre, who had come to say good-bye.

Jack didn't see that he had something under his gown, or that there were tears in the boy's eyes.

'Good-bye, Gray,' he said, wringing his hand; 'I'm so sorry! I'm——'

Something choked in his throat, and he could not get out another word; and the train began to move. He shut the door, and Jack saw him through an unwonted mist standing bare-headed on the platform, waving his cap.

The train steamed slowly out of the station, leaving all the old familiar things behind him: the old aims, the old ambitions, they were all slipping away from him as the train panted slowly out into the darkness. He could not bear to see the familiar landmarks slipping by; it was like leaving his life behind, and being borne away into a dark, unknown future. He put up his hand to his eyes to shut out the sight, and he was startled by feeling the touch of a cold nose against his face; and something was licking his hand.

Little Blantyre had brought Peter.

# CHAPTER XXXI.

### A DEBATE AT NEWNHAM.

'Long have all things been misgoverned by the foolish race
  of men,
Who've monopolized sword, sceptre, mitre, quiver, spade,
  and pen.
All the failures, all the follies, that the weary world bewails,
Have arisen, trust me, simply from the government of
  males.'

MOLLY was no longer expectant. She knew the worst. There was no longer any loophole for hope — there hadn't been from the first; but still, being only human—very human—she had nursed a secret hope that it would all come right in the end, that her lover's innocence would be triumphantly established.

It only made the shock worse when it came. She would have liked to sit down and have a good cry when she got back to her room; but she didn't feel the least like crying. She felt inordinately hungry. It was still a long time off hall time, and she could not remember ever having wanted her dinner so much. She recollected that somebody had given her a box of chocolates; they didn't look the least appetizing, but she took them out, and ate them slowly, one by one.

It was all very well eating up a box of chocolates as a balm for wounded feelings, but Molly couldn't put any spirit into it, and they were not at all satisfying.

It was quite a relief when the dinner-bell rang. She began with the soup, and went steadily through the *menu;* but the strangest thing of all was, that she felt quite as hungry after the dinner as before it. She began to realize that there is a hunger, a *craving*, rather, that food cannot satisfy, nor chocolates touch.

There was no time for reasoning on this strange thing, this new sensation; there was no time, indeed, for anything after hall.

The tables had to be hastily cleared out of the way, and the seats all rearranged, and the big dining-hall made ready for a debate.

There was no time for anything but to dress: to put a knot of flowers cunningly on her shoulder, or at her slender waist—all waists are supposed to be slender; perhaps, to put a flower in her hair—it was quite sure to tumble out before the evening was over; and to get into a pair of long gloves. Molly had barely time to get into her pink gown, and to put on her gloves, before the debate began; she didn't wear any flowers in her bosom to-night, and she hadn't stuck a rose in her hair.

She met a lot of girls, in their low evening gowns, shivering in that draughty passage that leads from the students' rooms to the Hall, but she stopped on her way to call for Dorothy Piggott, so that they all got in before her.

Dorothy Piggott, who was vice-president of the Newnham Debating Society, had already gone in, and Molly was the last to arrive.

Everybody was in her place when Molly came into the hall, and everybody turned round and looked at her. Everyone present knew of her trouble, and everyone looked at her curiously.

She nodded to her immediate friends in more than her usual sprightly manner, and took her seat at the further end of the hall —all the other seats were filled up—without betraying any sign of wanting sympathy or condolence from anybody.

It was exactly as a girl should behave who knows what is due to her, and was quite worthy of a member of a woman's college.

A great change had taken place in the aspect of the hall since dinner. On a raised daïs at the end of the great white hall, corresponding to the high table of a college hall, luxurious chairs were arranged for the president and vice-president of the debate and the tellers. Screens artistically draped were placed as a background to the group, and threw up in relief the dainty toilettes, which would have been completely lost against the cold white wall.

Tall palms and ferns were grouped effectively round the steps of the daïs, and on either side down the body of the hall were arranged wicker couches and seats for the supporters and opposers of the motion.

Every seat was full, and the low ripple of girlish laughter was suddenly hushed and the murmur of voices ceased as the vice-president took her seat, while—

'Through the illumined hall
Long lanes of splendour slanted o'er a press

Of snowy shoulders, thick as herded ewes,
And rainbow robes, and gems, and gem-like eyes,
And gold and golden heads; they to and fro
Fluctuated, as flowers in storm, some red, some pale,
All open-mouth'd.'

The vice-president, looking a little pale from her recent illness, rose amid a storm of applause. The members of the women's colleges are loyalty itself, and Dorothy Piggott was the brightest star on the Newnham horizon.

She looked like a star to-night in her 'April daffodil' gown, with her gleaming arms, and her pretty white neck, and something shining in her hair. What she lacked in stature she gained in train. A vice-president ought to look dignified, and Miss Piggott's daffodil train added quite a cubit to her stature.

Nobody at Molly's end of the room heard what she said, though she said it very nicely. When she sat down, a little bit of a girl that nobody could see rose from one of the side-benches and read the motion of the evening.

There was a general cry of 'Speak up' from the lower end of the room, and she read it over again a trifle louder. It really required a second reading.

The motion ran thus: 'That this house views with satisfaction the decline of masculine despotism.'

The motion was greeted with shouts of applause—and a little laughter.

'The speaker,' in a delightful girlish voice, with not a quake or a tremor in it, prefaced her remarks with some account of the recent victories gained by women. She gave a graphic description of the 'Siege of Cambridge.'

'It began,' she reminded her hearers, 'in '72, when a woman's college effected a lodgment on a hill not two miles out of Cambridge. Two years later Fort Newnham was occupied' (the applause at this statement was tremendous). 'Now the streets of Cambridge and the lecture-rooms were filled with women with note-books ; and soon, very soon, the academic gown and cap would be a necessary part of the wardrobe of every female undergraduate' (cries of 'Hear, hear !'). 'They were assumed even now—for photographic purposes—but the time was not far distant when it would be imperative to wear them. Not necessarily rusty, or in a fragmentary condition, but neat, and well brushed, and entire' (derisive cheers). 'And the cap of the undergraduate of the women's colleges would not be the limp, disreputable rag it now is, with all the backbone taken out of it, but a four-cornered parallelogram, with a becoming tassel, that would delight the hearts of Proctors' ('Hear, hear !' and cheers). 'The battle of the Tripos,' she further reminded them, 'was won in '81, and since that memorable date the roll of University distinction had year after year included the names of women in every branch of learning, ever creeping higher and higher, until the crowning success that had so recently placed a woman's name very near the head of the lists' (immense excitement and cheering. One or two girls pricked each other with knitting-needles, but that had nothing to do with the debate).

The opener was warming up, and her cheeks were flushed, and her bosom heaving beneath its costly lace, and no doubt her finger-tips were glowing, only one couldn't see them under her gloves.

She went on in the most animated way, showing that, however slowly, yet surely women were beginning to fill the prominent positions hitherto monopolized by men.

The opener of the debate sat down amid great cheering. If a man had been present he would have wept.

A girl—who, it was rumoured, was engaged to be married—a delightful girl in pink, jumped up directly the opener sat down and addressed the chair in ringing accents as 'Madam.' She deplored the course the hon. opener had taken. She begged the house to consider that woman was not intended as a rival, but as a companion to man (sensation. A voice: 'Speak for yourself!'). 'She spoke for herself,' she replied, rather tartly, 'and for that large class of women whose birthright was at stake—the birthright of love and reverence' (cries of 'Oh, oh!'). 'That precious birthright they were willing to barter for a paltry mess of University distinction and political pottage' (great sensation, and cries of 'Oh, oh!' and the hon. opposer sat down covered with well-deserved obloquy).

A lovely Amazon in a tightly-fitting white bodice, that showed her magnificent figure and the biceps of her bare white arms, stood up amid a murmur of applause. There was no need to ask her to 'speak up'; every word of her clear, perfectly-modulated voice could be heard at the further end of the hall and up in the white gallery above, where the girls were looking down, and dropping flowers upon the heads of the girls beneath.

She slew the last speaker in a few trenchant words. 'It made her boil over,' she said, 'to hear such idiotic remarks made by a member of a woman's college. The time was not far distant,' she predicted, 'when the woman of the future would dispute not only the supremacy on the river, but in the cricket and the football fields with men. It might be even necessary or expedient to adopt articles of attire hitherto monopolized by men. If they were found becoming as well as convenient, their universal adoption was inevitable. The world was ripening for a change; but'—she admitted with a sigh—'it was not *quite* ripe' ('Hear, hear!' and applause).

A pretty girl in glasses rose to ask the hon. opener if the increased liberty of women meant the less liberty of men. If so, she should oppose the motion on that ground. 'You see,' she remarked naïvely, 'we have to choose a companion from the sex, and we should not like him to be a nonentity' (subdued murmurs of applause).

And so, one by one, the sweet girl graduates, with golden hair or brown—to say nothing of gray—rose and expressed their views on this startling theme. There was no stammering or hesitation; there was not a girl in the room that hadn't got an opinion and didn't know how to express it. Except, indeed, Molly, and she sat in one of the back rows listening, but unheeding, with a red spot burning on either cheek, and cold shivers running down her back.

Perhaps it was the hall, for it was dreadfully draughty.

A girl behind her saw her shivering, and immediately began to tickle her bare shoulders with the feathers of her fan; while another girl took her hairpins out; and a third threw down a shower of rose-leaves on her from the gallery above.

It was one way of showing sympathy.

She didn't make much of the debate, though she listened with a pertinacity that was almost terrible.

She heard a confused murmur, an endless repetition of such stock phrases as 'Madam,' 'Hon. Opener,' 'Hon. Opposer,' 'This house,' and once she heard somebody warned not to be 'cock-sure.'

She rose up with a vague impression that it had been definitely arranged that there was to be a female Vice-Chancellor; that the examiners and moderators for the Tripos were to be women; and that a lady had been chosen to preach the University sermon.

The house divided on the close of the debate with an overwhelming majority for the motion.

After the debate the middle of the hall was rapidly cleared, and dancing began. It was quite a sight to behold nearly two hundred girls supporting each other through the mazes of the waltz—they affect waltzes at Newnham, independent of the support of the masculine arm.

There might not have been a man in creation, to see the way those girls ignored his existence. The men were not even missed.

Nobody sighed for Selwyn, and nobody wept for Ridley—at least, not audibly. '

Molly had no heart for dancing. Her heart was cold within her, and her feet were like lead.

She slipped away when there was no one to

notice her, and shut herself up in her own room. She couldn't understand the change that had come over her.

She had always looked upon happiness as her due, and she could not understand anything coming in the way of it.

Oh, it was a dreadful awakening!

But she didn't awake all at once; a numbed, miserable feeling possessed her, and she only felt that all the warmth and sunshine had gone out of her life.

She would go on living, she told herself; probably she would live to be a very old woman—grief like hers didn't kill, but it worked changes; it altered the whole course of life. She was sure she was going to be a very different person in the future. Probably she would do a great deal of good.

She thought of all these things while she was undressing. She did not think of them coherently; she had a vague consciousness that the Molly of yesterday was not the Molly of to-day, that she would have to be dealt with differently.

She even folded up her pink gown with a feeling that she could never put it on again. She folded it up very carefully, nevertheless.

She pictured herself like St. Christina, as she stripped off her trinkets—her little silver bangles and her bead necklace, and a trumpery little garnet ring — renouncing the world with its pomps and vanities. and that henceforth she was going to dress very plainly (she was going to look perfectly hideous), and devote her life to good works. She was going to do a good many. and she was going to do them very secretly. They would not be found out till she was dead, and then—and then she would like to come to life again and hear what nice things people said about them—especially what Keith Fellowes said.

She went to bed thinking all this nonsense; but she couldn't go to sleep. She heard the hours strike one after the other, and still sleep would not come, only the dreary round of memory recalling every incident of the past dreadful week. She never could remember her Greek grammar an hour after she had learnt it ; but here was memory, patient and painstaking, recalling every incident of that terrible interview, even to the hateful *frou-frou* of the silk lining of that woman's gown.

Molly could bear it no longer: she got out of bed and struck a light.

There was a little syringe, charged with morphia, that a girl who was suffering from neuralgia had left in her room, on the table beside the candlestick. Her eye fell upon it as she struck the light. She took it up curiously, with that dreadful yearning for temporary oblivion and rest. Should she use it?

She had seen the other girls use it often enough, when racked with neuralgia and nervous headaches.

At any rate, it would clog the wheels of memory, and dull that aching pain at her heart.

She pricked it in her arm, as she had seen the other girls do, and she injected the morphia. She had no idea how much she ought to inject, and she injected it freely, and then, feeling that she was getting stupid, she blew out the candle and went to bed.

But it didn't bring the relief she sought; it only made her feel stupider and stupider. Then her head began to turn round, and something choked in her throat, and her heart stopped—or something like it—and a dreadful feeling seized her that she was dying—suffocating here in this stifling room, like a rat in a hole.

She never knew how she got out of bed and

crawled to the window. She only remembered the feeling of the cool night air on her brow. She had thrown the window wide open, but she was too weak to stand, and she sank down on the low window-ledge, where she was accustomed to sit, leaning for support against the woodwork, and her arms falling helplessly by her side. And she remembered no more.

## CHAPTER XXXII.

### A WINTER NIGHT'S TALE.

'And no one but the baby cried for poor Lorraine, Lorèe!'

DOROTHY PIGGOTT slept like a top. No one has explained why tops are supposed to sleep well. Tops usually wobble when they are said to be going to sleep. Miss Piggott did not wobble: she lay calm and placid, with a smile on her lip, and Mr. Brackenbury's letter under her pillow.

Her room was beneath Molly's; but she slept so soundly that she did not hear her get out of bed, and she did not hear the window open. She was in the middle of a beautiful dream. She dreamt she was riding a race—and winning it, too—with all the world looking on, and somebody was singing:

' You're booked to ride your capping race to-day at Coulterlee,
You're booked to ride Vindictive, for all the world to see ;
To keep him straight, to keep him first, and win the run for me.'

She knew the voice well. She couldn't mistake it. It was Mr. Brackenbury's voice.

And then in the middle of the verse there was a thud—a dull, heavy thud, as if someone were thrown. But still the voice went on singing :

' Are you ready for your steeplechase, Lorraine, Lorraine, Lorèe ?
Barum, Barum, Barum, Barum, Barum, Barum, Baree !'

Would it never stop singing those senseless words ? They were not words, they were moans; there was a pain in every one of them.

' Barum—Barum—Baree !' Oh, how someone was moaning!

Still the song was ringing in her ears, and the sound of the voice was so familiar. It was not a man's voice now—it was hardly a woman's; it was like the cry of a child.

Of course, it was a baby crying! And again the words rang in her ears:

'And no one but the baby cried for poor Lorraine, Lorèe!'

Would it never stop crying?

It woke her at last with its pitiful moan, and her pillow was wet with tears. She dried her eyes and turned over to sleep again, and still someone was moaning.

She was wide awake now, and, sitting up in bed, listening with straining ears.

Yes, it *was* a human voice—a faint, weak cry as of someone in pain. It was not far off—it was quite near; and it was not—oh no, it was not a baby's voice!

She sat up, with a sudden panic at her heart, which was thumping dreadfully. Had burglars broken into the college? and were they murdering the inmates one by one?

Dorothy Piggott could bear it no longer. She crept out of bed, and, opening her door softly, peeped out into the corridor. Everything was quite still. There wasn't a sound, except a cricket chirping cheerfully in some remote region.

No, nobody was being murdered. She crept back to bed with a suspicion that she had been dreaming. It was an uncomfortable nightmare: it was that plum-cake she ate with her coffee.

There it was again! It was quite close now—only a few feet from her bed! It wasn't the plum-cake. She was close to the window, and the sound seemed to come from outside. She raised a corner of the blind and looked out. It was a dark night, and it was raining fast. She could see nothing at first, but presently, when her eyes got accustomed to the darkness, she saw—she was certain she saw—something white on the ground. A heap of white garments—a shapeless, snowy heap. Even while she looked the sound was repeated. O heaven! it came from the ground.

Dorothy Piggott hadn't an atom of courage, but she had what was quite as good, she had common-sense; and she fled down the corridor to Miss Godolphin's room and beat at her door.

'Oh, come — come quickly!' she cried, bursting into the room. She clung to Miss Godolphin's hands with piteous entreaty in her voice. 'Oh, come—come!'

'What is it?'

Miss Godolphin was always prepared for anything that might happen, and she was always cool; but it was difficult to keep cool when awoke suddenly out of sleep, and dragged against sense and reason along a dark corridor in the middle of the night. She didn't stay to put on anything, but went out into the cold passage as she was, barefooted, and in her thin white garments, gliding noiselessly along past the doors of all the sleeping rooms, with Dorothy Piggott clinging to her with that piteous cry : ' Come along ! Oh, do come along !'

Miss Godolphin did not need persuasion. She did come along as fast as anyone could with bare feet on those cold, cold stones.

' There !' said Dorothy Piggott, when they reached the door of her room—' there it is again !'

There it was, sure enough. Not the words of that mournful refrain, ' Barum—Barum—Baree!' not the piteous cry of poor Lorraine's baby. It was a human cry—a faint, low cry, with an agony of pain in it. It came from the direction of the window.

In a moment Miss Godolphin had thrown

the window open and was looking out into the night.

In the utter blackness and darkness without there was nothing visible but this snowy, shapeless heap on the grass. It might be some sheep that had wandered in through the open gate and were herded together for warmth; it might be some white garments that had fluttered down from some upper window; it might be—— Oh! it might be——

As Miss Godolphin stood at the open window, with these thoughts flashing through her mind, another low, weak moan was borne upon the air—it came from the white heap on the ground.

Miss Godolphin was not an athlete or an acrobat, and she had passed the agile period of her *première jeunesse,* and the windows at Newnham are some feet from the ground; but in a moment, before the girl who stood beside her knew what she was going to do, she had cleared the window and was bending over that white heap on the grass.

A moment of awful suspense and doubt, and then her cry rang through the night, ' O God ! it is a girl fallen out of window !'

She was stooping over her, and trying to raise her in her arms, but at the first movement the girl moaned and gave a quivering cry of anguish, and Miss Godolphin laid her back upon the grass.

'Quick, fetch someone ! Call the girls, send at once for a doctor ; she has broken some bones. Fly! fly! fly!'

There was no need to tell Dorothy Piggott to fly ; the wind couldn't have flown faster. She beat at the doors, she roused the girls wildly from their slumber, she tore the champion athlete of Newnham out of bed, and nearly shook her senses out of her to waken her.

'Get on some things; oh, do get on some

things quickly ! A girl has fallen out of window, and is dying on the grass ! Get on some things and fly for a doctor ! You will fetch him quicker than anyone ; bring him back with you. If ever you ran in your life, run now !'

The girl did not need to be adjured further. She flung on an ulster and a hat, and—yes, she did put on a pair of shoes—and throwing open her window, as the readiest mode of egress, she flew across the grass.

'Fly ! fly !' said Miss Godolphin, who caught sight of her flying by.

'Fly ! fly !' shouted a dozen voices of girls who had already reached the spot where the white moaning figure lay.

There really was no need of such invocations. Atalanta herself could not have flown faster ; and really, from the glimpses that could be obtained of white drapery beneath that dark ulster, and the gleaming ankles that were doing such good service, it *might* have been Atalanta herself.

There was quite a crowd of girls in Dorothy Piggott's room when she returned to it, and the passages were crowded with ghostly figures gliding noiselessly through them—not quite noiselessly, for there was a low murmur of voices. A hushed, awestricken murmur, and somebody was whispering a name.

Dorothy Piggott pushed her way through the crowd to the open window. The white heap was still there, and Miss Godolphin was still there in her white bending over her, and the girls were shivering around—and it was raining hard.

'Who is it?' she asked, and the question faltered on her lips. Who could it be, there, in that spot, but the girl who kept above her?

'It's Molly. Who else would do such a mad thing but Molly?'

It was Adela speaking, and she had on a

nice warm dressing-gown, and a woolly wrap over her head, and fur-lined slippers, and she kept carefully out of the draught.

'Molly! Oh, my poor dear!'

Miss Piggott would have got out of the window on to the wet grass, but the girls held her back by main force. She would not be pacified; she would not be kept back. She would carry her bedding and her pillows over to the open window and implore the girls outside to put them under Molly's head, and cover her with the blankets.

They dared not move her till the doctor came; the slightest attempt to lift her made her cry out in agony. Who could say what injury she had sustained? whether she would bear the lifting, or succumb in the effort to remove her?

There was nothing to be done but to let her lie there, as she had fallen, until skilled assistance came.

They covered her with blankets; she was wet through to the skin, but they could do nothing more. Through that long dreadful time, till help came, Miss Godolphin stood beside her. Someone brought a cloak and threw it around her; and another threw a shawl over her wet dishevelled head, but nobody thought about her feet.

She sent all the girls in—she would not let one of them stay; but she stood there herself, in the rain and the bitter cold of the December night, holding an umbrella over the poor moaning heap of clothes piled up on the grass, until the doctor came.

It was astonishing how soon he came; and yet the time had seemed so long!

Atalanta was there before him: she had waited for him, and brought him back with her, but she had outrun him in the race.

Gently, tenderly, under his direction, they moved the unconscious girl upon the grass, lifting her on a mattress through the window into Dorothy Piggott's room.

And then, while the doctor was finding out what had really happened to Molly, the girls led Miss Godolphin away.

They had to carry her in between them, for her numbed and stiffened limbs refused their office. She could not move an inch; she could only stand there, rigid and patient; and when her work was done, they had to carry her away.

Then, and not till then, they discovered that her feet were bare.

Some day, when an epic is written recounting the heroic acts of the women of the nineteenth century, the tale of this winter night will be told.

# CHAPTER XXXIII.

### GOOD-BYE !

WILLY-NILLY, everybody had gone down.

Whether he would or not, Jack had gone down. Like Dick Whittington, he had gone on his sorrowful way with a little dumb friend that licked his hand at every convenient opportunity ; only in his case it was a dog, and not a cat.

Mr. Brackenbury, too, had gone down prematurely. Nobody exactly knew why ; and he was not communicative on the point. The morning after Jack's ignoble flight he was summoned before a meeting of the college authorities. Whatever transpired at that meeting, the result of it was that Mr. Brackenbury was rusticated.

It only wanted a few days to the end of the term, but these few days he was not allowed to keep. He was sent down at once.

This was his third year, and the men of his standing, and the college generally, bore his rustication with great equanimity.

No one came to wish him good-bye but some duns, who had in some mysterious way got scent of his hurried departure. Coming in during the day, he caught sight from below of the crowd that had gathered on his staircase —a noisy, threatening crowd that might have appalled the stoutest heart.

Mr. Brackenbury laughed his delightful little low laugh when he saw them gathered there outside his oak, and turned back into the quad, and went up another staircase into another man's rooms that looked out on the leads. Thence communication with his own rooms was easy enough, and if he didn't know the way, Smiler was there, ready to show him.

He knew it quite well, however; it was the way he had used with such a happy result on that memorable fifth of November when he ran into the senior tutor's arms at the bottom of the staircase, thus clearly proving to him that he could not have been in his own rooms when the cracker was flung at him from the window.

He completed all his preparations in the most leisurely way, while the crowd grumbled behind the door; and when he had quite finished, he went down into the court below by the way he came. He patted Smiler affectionately before he went, and congratulated himself that it wasn't his bedmaker, and that he didn't ask him for a tip.

By this simple ruse he had escaped his gyp, and his bedmaker, and the hungry army of college servants. He sauntered across the quad and hailed a hansom, and drove to the station, and when he reached Liverpool Street he wired back to Cambridge for his luggage to be sent after him.

It was very neatly done.

The Junior Dean had gone down. He, too, had left Cambridge to return no more. He was not rusticated. He had not lost his fellowship. Nothing had happened to disturb his relations with the authorities of his college. He never knew the attitude the dons of St. Stephen's took after that miserable scene in Jack's rooms. He was too ill to know anything about it until it had nearly blown over. Mr. Flynt had been his champion, and fought his battle for him in the college combination room, when the matter was discussed after Hall; but he had never breathed a word to him about it.

It was not until he was up again once more, and walking feebly enough through the streets of Cambridge, that he learned something of the esteem in which men held him. He did not notice at first the cold looks of the men he met; he did not observe that undergraduates who used to cap him passed him by unheeding. He was so preoccupied that only when a murmur arose in a street near his college, where a number of men where returning from Hall, was his attention arrested.

The murmur grew louder, and some men threw up their windows and began to hiss and hoot in a most extraordinary way.

The Junior Dean paused and looked round, and looked up at the men's faces at the windows with a bewildered air. This was a signal for renewed hisses, and presently the murmur had risen to a roar, and someone— he never knew who—threw a missile at him.

Then it dawned upon him that the men were hooting him!

He flushed crimson, and his lip began to twitch, and he limped slowly away towards his college gate.

He went down the next day. He could bear anything but this—to be hooted in the streets of his own beloved University!

The unlucky day on which the Junior Dean took that memorable walk through the streets of his dear old Cambridge was a few days after Molly's accident. He had heard of it; everybody had heard of it; and he had called upon Mrs. Gray for news of her niece, but Mrs. Gray had refused to see him.

He had turned away from that familiar door with a bleeding heart, and walked in another direction that was also familiar. He thought he might as well get it over all at once. He went direct from Mrs. Gray's to the house where he was to have taken his bride.

Of course it had been given up directly the engagement was at an end; and all the chairs and rugs, and dainty things that Molly had bought for the drawing-room, and the pots and pans she had wasted so much arithmetic over for the kitchen, were sold by public auction at the Corn Exchange, and the gyps and lodging-house-keepers had bought them for a song.

The Junior Dean had never paid for them, and he hadn't the courage to send the cheque for that hundred pounds to Mrs. Gray now. He had a conviction that if he sent it it would be indignantly returned.

The house had been let again to a Fellow of a college who had recently married, and it was already occupied. He stood in the chill December dusk looking up at it, with a mute agony at his heart; and even as he stood there, with the bleak wintry wind shivering in the leafless lime-trees overhead, he remarked that the rattling old Venetian blind was still a little aslant; and by the lights in the basement he saw that the new kitchen-range was cooking the dinner of the new tenant.

The subtle aroma of that other Fellow's baked meats came to him as he stood there, and he turned away with a groan.

This was the last straw!

He remembered how Molly was whispering to him behind her fan about that kitchen-range on that last night of their happiness. It was the last thing he remembered; and then had followed the dreadful scene of the morrow, with all its miserable results: his own illness; the wretched scandal; the breaking off the engagement; and now this accident of Molly's. He never learnt the truth about the accident. He heard, as everybody else in Cambridge heard, that Molly had been suffering from neuralgia, and that she had taken an anodyne for it, and had accidentally taken an overdose, and opening the window for air, the ledge being low, she had fallen out.

He had to be satisfied with these few crumbs of information about the woman he loved. He never knew how much he loved her till she fell out of window and was nearly lost to him, and to this world, for ever.

This accident of Molly's gave him an excuse —no, not an excuse, an additional reason—for having her name on his lips whenever he went into that Presence Chamber that he was wont to seek.

It took him there now more than ever. It was all he could do. He couldn't write to her with that disabled right arm that hung helplessly by his side. He could send no message to her: he had been distinctly requested by her father to hold no further communication with her. There was only one thing left for him to do—to pray for her.

Nine girls out of ten would have been killed outright by that ugly fall, or would have died from the effects of the exposure on that wet winter night; but Molly wasn't a dying sort.

She used to tell herself that she had as many lives as a cat, and this incident confirmed the statement. Only a cat could have fallen from that height and received less injury.

She had broken a collar-bone, and dislocated one or two other bones, but she had sustained no vital injury.

The broken bone and the dislocations kept her up at Newnham after the other girls had gone down. Adela, who stayed up to take her back, had a gay time in Cambridge during the weeks of her enforced residence. It was the season for balls, and concerts, and Christmas festivities, and Adela stayed up with the best grace in the world. There wasn't anything going on in Devonshire, and just now the house was particularly gloomy on account of Jack's disgrace.

Dorothy Piggott was the last of the girls to go down. She stayed behind till Molly was quite out of danger. She begged very hard to be allowed to stay up to nurse her, but Miss Godolphin wouldn't hear of it. There was that other Tripos coming on, and the credit of the women's colleges was at stake, and the short Christmas vacation was not a minute too long to prepare for that fierce ordeal that awaited her.

The night before she went down, she lingered late in Molly's room. They had so much to say to each other, and it was their last night. Molly recollected then, almost for the first time since her accident, Jack's warning about Mr. Brackenbury, and she said what she could.

'Is it gone too far, Dolly,' she asked, as Dorothy Piggott bent over her to say goodnight; 'is it gone too far to draw back? Have you really promised to marry him?'

They had been talking about Mr. Brackenbury, and Dorothy Piggott had been showing Molly his likeness.

'Gone too far?' she repeated, with a delightful flush on her cheeks; 'what do you mean, Molly? You don't think I'm going to play fast and loose like——'

'Like me, I suppose you mean,' interrupted Molly impatiently, and with a hasty movement that made her give a little cry, and turn her face to the pillow.

'I didn't say you, though I think you've behaved shamefully. I should have trusted Neil if he had been in Mr. Fellowes' place. I should have believed his word against any accusations a wicked woman brought against him;' and she looked fondly down at the portrait in her hand.

It didn't look exactly a face to be trusted. The pensive lips in Mr. Brackenbury's counterfeit presentment had a little curl at the corners, and there was an unmistakable twinkle in the eyes that all the wily photographer's skill couldn't keep out of them.

Still, it was a face that women loved to look upon, wherever the charm lay. Perhaps it was the twinkle?

'Oh, you poor dear!' said Molly, watching her, and remembering Jack's words; 'he's not half good enough for you. You—you ought to marry a man like Keith, like Keith was—a man you could fall down and worship. You couldn't find anything noble in Mr. Brackenbury to worship. You couldn't make an ideal of him. You couldn't even put him on a pedestal.'

'No,' said Dorothy Piggott, smiling; 'I shouldn't think of putting him on a pedestal. I am quite content with him as he is. He isn't Keith Fellowes—I don't think I should have cared for him if he had been: we don't love the Gods, we worship them. He is Neil

Brackenbury—and I am quite content with him—and I have promised to marry him.'

There was nothing more to be said. Dorothy Piggott knew all about her lover. She knew that he had been sent down. She knew that he could not take a degree. She knew that he was deeply in debt, that he had mortgaged his patrimony. Above all, she knew, perhaps instinctively, that in the race of life she would be the runner, not he. She accepted him with all these things against him, and, if the truth must be told, was glad to get him.

Justice isn't half so blind as love; but she has a sword and can avenge herself.

Molly travelled down to Devonshire during the first week of the new year. It was the dreariest, dismallest January morning when she left Cambridge. One of the wet fen fogs had been hanging about for days, and the trees and hedges were dripping in a sad, spiritless way as she bid adieu to Newnham. She could not bear to look out of the window of the fly that took her to the station.

She could not see all the old familiar places without recalling that glad, glad day when she had come up—when the sun was shining, and her heart of bliss was full to the brim. It was empty now, and desolate, and great blobs of moisture, like tears, were shaken from the branches overhead, and rolled down the carriage windows.

Molly looked sadly across the intervening gulf in that miserable drive, and mutely asked herself if she were the same girl who had driven gaily through the busy street in a hansom on that far-off day.

She seemed to have bidden herself—the old happy Molly—good-bye. She could not look back on her old unreasonable happiness now without wonder. How could she ever have expected it to last?

It was about as miserable a journey down to Devonshire as it could be at that time in the year. The fog gave place to a cruel north wind that brought the feathery snowflakes with it. It was bitter cold, and Adela monopolized the lion's share of the wraps and the foot-warmer.

Molly was feeling miserably weak, and, do what she would, she could not keep a few small tears from running down her cheeks, and she dared not wipe them away, for Adela was watching her furtively above the top of her newspaper.

It was a miserable home-coming. The dog-cart was waiting for the girls at the junction station, and they had to drive back in the teeth of that bitter wind with the snow driving in their faces. They expected that Jack would have met them at the station; but there was no Jack, only the stable-boy, and he had come away without any wraps or even a foot-warmer.

It was a cruel ride back; but Adela was so considerate as to give up the front seat to Molly: it was easier for her to get up to, only she had the wind and the snow in her face all the way.

The few small tears could flow unobserved now, and she was so utterly weak and miserable that she cried all the way back from the station. She was white all over, as if she had been a snow-wreath, when the dog-cart stopped at the Rectory door.

There was no one to welcome the girls but Madge; and when Molly felt her motherly arms once more around her, she was so weak, and cold, and miserable, that she forgot all about Adela, and began to cry hysterically on her tender bosom.

Madge took off her wet things, and drew her over to the blazing hearth, and comforted her as she used to comfort her in her passionate fits of weeping as a child.

'Where's papa? and why didn't Jack come to meet us?' Adela asked, looking suspiciously round the homely old room, over which a shadow seemed to have fallen. Madge shook her head, and pointed significantly to Molly.

'Papa is in his study,' she said in a whisper; 'he seldom leaves it now; and Jack —Jack is over there,' and she nodded in the direction of the door.

'Over where?' said Molly, looking up; she had overheard the whisper.

'Never mind, dear, where he is for to-night. Why, I declare, you are wet quite through! Come off to-bed at once.'

'I won't stir till you tell me where Jack is,' said Molly with something of her old spirit. 'I know there is some mystery about Jack. I have heard nothing about him since he was sent down.'

'Not now, dear; wait till to-morrow

morning. Have a good night's rest, and then you shall hear all the home news.'

'I can't wait till to-morrow morning; I must hear now. Good heavens, Madge! he —he isn't dead?'

'No, no, no! Thank God! it is not so bad as that. It's as bad almost as it can be —but not that. He's over at the Golden Lion. He's there night and day—and—and I think he's broken papa's heart!'

## CHAPTER XXXIV.

### A SAD HOME-COMING.

MADGE hadn't at all exaggerated the case. Jack had been going to the bad ever since he came home.

It was a dreadful home-coming. Every man who has been sent down, for even a term or two, knows something of the reception that awaits him on such occasions.

After the first shock the Rector shut himself up in his study. He could not bear that anyone should look upon his grief. It had come to him so suddenly, at a moment when he was building upon a brilliant future for Jack. He had only two more terms to keep, and then, he told himself—he told everybody, indeed—Jack would carry away the highest honours the University had to offer.

He had even planned a visit to Cambridge, in order to be present on that proud and happy day when Jack should take his high degree amid the applause of the crowded Senate House.

He had pictured the scene dozens of times; and now—now, while the disappointment was so keen, while the wound was fresh, he shut himself up in his study and refused to see anyone. He nursed his bitterness in that gloomy study by recalling over and over again the many plans he had made for Jack's future, and the sacrifices he had been making for him all his life.

Jack skulked moodily about the house and the Rectory grounds during those first dreary days, with Peter ever following at his heels, in the expectation that his father would relent.

He had always relented before, however grievous the provocation. Surely he would relent now! His heart was full of remorse and tenderness for the old man, and he wept the bitterest tears on his pillow on that first night he had ever shed in his life. Nobody but Peter witnessed these agonies of repentance and remorse, and he was always ready to lick his hand, or his tears, despite their saltness. He could not have lived, he told himself, through that unhappy time without Peter.

If the Rector had relented, if he had taken the prodigal to his bosom, like the wise father in the parable, he had won his son. At that moment of bitter remorse, of real repentance, Jack's heart was so softened that he would have gladly humbled himself, and poured out all his sorry confession like the prodigal upon his father's bosom.

He had the same confession to make, and he might have made it in the same words :

'Father, I have sinned against heaven, and before thee, and am no more worthy to be called thy son.'

But the Rector shut himself up in his study.

There was no fatted calf killed when Jack came home ; there was no best robe brought out, not even a pair of shoes for his feet—and he wanted a pair sadly—there was nothing to break down that bitter resistance in his heart.

One word of compassion and forgiveness would have melted all his reserve, and he would have told his father that miserable story about the bill that was coming due.

But the Rector shut himself up in his study, and the softening moment was lost.

Jack skulked about the village for the first week, fancying everybody was looking at him and knew of his disgrace. He was not only miserable and ashamed, but there was the anxiety about that horrible bill ever gnawing at his heart.

His gloomy face soon began to be seen in the taproom of the Golden Lion. He slunk away from his equals, but he did not mind meeting the company in the taproom of the village inn. He was always sure of a welcome there, and the best seat on the old black settle by the fire. There was warmth, and welcome, and company, albeit rough company, here; while at the Rectory, over the way, there was nothing but silence and gloom.

These visits to the Golden Lion had grown more frequent lately as the time drew on for the bill to become due. He lived in that foul, heated atmosphere, reeking with fumes of liquor and stale tobacco, from morning till night; it was the only place in which he could forget that miserable bill.

The Rector never asked for him, and no one ventured to tell him how Jack, his hope and pride, now spent his days, and so the miserable time had worn on till the girls came back.

Jack was not down to breakfast when Molly came down the next morning.

Nobody but Adela inquired for him, and Madge hurriedly replied, with an appealing glance in the direction of her father, that he was not up.

Molly was shocked at the change the last few weeks had wrought in her father.

His hair had grown grayer, and there were two upright lines on his face she had never seen there before, and his eyes were certainly a good deal farther back than they used to be. He kissed his daughters, but he hadn't very much to say to them. He never referred to Molly's engagement, and he did not mention her lover's name.

' You have brought all your things away ?' he said, when she happened to speak about Newnham and the kindness that she had received there; ' you are not going back ?'

' Yes, papa,' she said humbly ; 'I have brought everything away. I have no wish to go back.'

And then her eyes filled with tears, and she had to turn hastily away to keep him from seeing them.

She didn't see Jack till quite the middle of the day, when she came upon him in the old schoolroom where they used to learn their lessons together when they were children.

A newly-lighted fire was spluttering in the grate, and his breakfast had been laid there. Madge dared not let it wait for him in the dining-room, in case the Rector should come in.

' Oh, Jack !' said Molly, coming over to

him with quite a flush of anger on her face. She was quite prepared to give him a good scolding, but something in his face stopped her, and she paused and looked at him, and then, in the most inconsequent way, she threw her arms around him and began crying on his shoulder.

It was so utterly unlike Molly to cry; he didn't remember having seen her in tears since the old passionate days of her childhood, when storms were of frequent occurrence.

She was weakened by her accident, and her nerves had been shaken, he told himself, as he kissed her in brotherly fashion, and disengaged himself as quickly as he could from her clinging embrace, and returned to his breakfast. But this had nothing to do with Molly's tears. It was something she saw in his face that broke her down.

'Oh, Jack!' she said humbly, 'I'm so sorry.'

'Yes,' he said, chipping his egg; 'I'm awfully sorry. I'm more sorry for the poor old governor than I am for myself. Poor old governor!'

'It isn't that, Jack. It isn't the being sent down—other men are sent down—it's the disgrace you are bringing upon us—upon him. I thought you were braver, Jack; that you wouldn't give in so easily. This — this disgrace, here, in our own parish, is worse, a thousand times worse, than being sent down.'

Jack groaned, and pushed his egg away untasted.

'You don't know all, Molly,' he said with a catch in his voice; 'you don't know what's driving me to it. If you knew all you'd understand.'

'All? What have you done, Jack?'

'Done!' said Jack bitterly—'you'll know soon enough. I've done about the cursedest bit of folly that ever any poor beggar was led into. I'd better have thrown myself into the Cam: it would have been a better day's work, and have saved you all the trouble and disgrace.'

'Trouble and disgrace?' Molly repeated with a whitening face, and a strange sinking at her heart. There had been trouble and disgrace enough already; what more could there be?

'It's that Mr. Brackenbury,' she said presently, with a catch in her breath, and her brows drawn together.

'Yes,' said Jack moodily, 'you're not far wrong. It's that devil Brackenbury;' and then he rose up and went to the schoolroom window and drummed upon it, as he used to drum upon it when he was a boy.

'What have you done, Jack? Tell me, what has he made you do?' Molly asked fearfully, with that sick feeling at her heart.

She came over and stood beside him,

looking out of the window they had so often looked out of in their childhood, into the old familiar garden.

Everything was unchanged: the same sloping lawn, with the rose-bushes in the borders, and the fruit-trees, and the shrubs, and the high laurel hedge. They were all covered with snow now, and the lawn was one unbroken sheet of white; and looking down from that window, Molly recalled the time when there were little footprints in it, and she and Jack used to pelt each other with snowballs, on that very spot. She fancied she could see the little footmarks now, and the memory of that old time made her put her hand caressingly on Jack's shoulder and implore him to tell her what this disgrace that threatened him was.

'You will know soon enough,' he said moodily, and then he shook off her clinging hand and went out of the room.

If he had remembered those little footprints in the snow he might have told her ; he used to tell her everything in those old days.

He looked so gloomy when he left the room that Molly had a dreadful fear on her mind that he was going to drown himself in the dark rapid stream that skirted the meadows beyond the Rectory lawn.

She stood looking out of the window, in the direction of the dark water, so dark in the white landscape, like a black ribbon winding through the white fields.

But Jack had not gone in the direction of the river ; he had slunk out the back way, and gone across the village street to the Golden Lion.

It wasn't a stone's-throw from the Rectory ; only the broad rambling village street divided them, and anyone slipping out by that back entrance could reach it unobserved.

It was a miserable hopeless day, with the

snow falling, and the wind moaning round the house in an eerie way it had when it happened to be in a certain quarter.

There was a dreary pallor in all the rooms, reflected from the white landscape without, that no warmth of blazing fires could make cheerful. The girls drew round the fire in the old home parlour and talked in low tones while the snow fell thickly without, or the fitful wind carried it in whirling eddies against the window-pane. They had nothing cheerful to talk about as they sat there; only loss, and disappointment, and pain—quite everyday subjects, the common experience, but they were new to Molly.

They might have talked about Adela's approaching marriage, but Adela was not communicative. It was not at all settled when it was to be; certainly not until the Tripos examinations were over, until the long vacation. 'She didn't like things talked about so long beforehand,' she said in her superior way, which shut Molly and poor timid little Madge up. Of course, Molly knew that the snub was meant for her.

Oh, how they had talked about the Junior Dean !

There was not a girl for miles round that did not know that he limped, to say the least of it ; but there wasn't a soul in Silverton who had been favoured with the most meagre personal details of Adela's betrothed, except, indeed, Madge, who had caught a glimpse of that portrait with a fringe.

' I wouldn't marry him if there was not another man in the world !' Molly had told Madge confidentially.

Other girls, doubtless, said the same ; but he hadn't given them the opportunity of accepting him, which perhaps accounted for it.

There was very little said about Molly's engagement and her lover's unfaithfulness. It seemed quite an old story; all the wonder of it had died out. There was no use in talking about it—it was like opening up an old wound. Madge had had a little tragedy in her own life, and she could feel for her younger sister.

Nobody had ever heard anything about it, it had been such a quiet tragedy. It had happened years ago, when the younger girls were quite little. A curate had been taking temporary charge of the parish while her father was absent for a summer holiday, and he naturally came very much in her way. She had not seen many young men in her lifetime, and her heart was fresh and green, and quite ready for young Love to take root in it. Before she knew it, Madge—the mother of these motherless girls, the mainstay of her widowed father's house—was in love.

There was nothing to be done, she told herself when she made the awful discovery, but to get out as fast as she had got in. The task was not so easy ; and to make it more difficult, the curate proposed to her the very next day.

There was only one word to be said—' No ! no ! no !'

She said it firmly. She didn't even tell him that she cared just a little bit for him. He might not have gone so easily if she had.

She received his simple, manly declaration with the cruellest assumption of indifference.

' You do not love me ?' he said, turning very pale.

' No, no ! indeed I do not.'

' Not—not in the least ?' he went on desperately.

' Not in the least.'

He looked at her as she stood beside her work-table, pale and self-possessed, not agitated—only a little distressed—with a grave reproach in his kind eyes that haunted her for years after.

He made no further appeal; he went out and left her standing there, white and cool—while every nerve was in an agony and her heart was bleeding.

The Rector returned to his charge the next day, and the curate packed up his belongings and left the village.

Madge never breathed a word of what had happened to anybody. She didn't know that she had been guilty of an unselfish piece of heroism—she only knew what it cost her.

There were lines on her face that shouldn't have been on a woman's face under thirty. Perhaps they were caused by poring over the butcher's book, and keeping the accounts of the village clubs. Everybody put them down to these meaner household cares that mar in time the fairest faces. But it wasn't the butcher's book that made that little pucker under her eyes that was so visible in the sunshine.

The dullest faces would not be devoid of interest if we knew the sad little stories the unlovely lines and wrinkles tell.

Molly had never heard of her sister's lover. She often wondered why she read the *Record* so persistently. For her own part, she never could read it without yawning, and Madge scanned it eagerly week after week, as if she were searching for something—something she had lost—and couldn't find it.

Jack did not appear at dinner, on that first day of their home-coming ; nor did he put in an appearance at their early afternoon tea, or the eight o'clock supper, and the prayers that followed it. Nobody inquired for him, and except for the girls exchanging glances across the table he wasn't missed. The Rector did not mention his name. If he knew where his son was, where he spent his days and nights, he gave no sign.

When prayers were over he kissed the girls

in his cold, formal manner, and went back to his study.

The house was shut up, and the servants went to bed, and the dining-room fire burnt low, and still Jack did not return.

'Go to bed, Molly,' said Madge, when the clock had done striking, and she heard the study door open. 'Papa will be angry if he sees you here; go to bed at once.'

'And you?' said Molly in a whisper. 'What will you do?'

'I? Oh, I wait up for him in the kitchen.'

Madge put out the lamp, and reassuring herself that the embers in the grate were safely dying out, she crept softly out of the dining-room by another door into the kitchen.

Molly followed her, and as the girls stood in the dark stone passage between the kitchen and the room they had left, they heard their father try the fastenings of the front-door and the shutters of the dining-room, and by-

and-by the sound of his slow, heavy footsteps ascending the stairs ; and then all was silent.

Madge raked together the embers in the kitchen grate, and put on some half-charred logs, and the girls nestled together in a corner of the wide chimney waiting for the unhappy brother who was once their dearest pride.

'Oh, Madge!' sobbed Molly on her sister's shoulder. 'Do you do this every night?'

'Hush ! darling. Yes, every night. I don't know what would happen if Jack were to come home and find the doors closed against him. Perhaps he would never come again.'

'And doesn't papa know?'

'Sometimes I think he knows. He goes round the house and shuts all up, and sees to the fastenings every night before he goes to bed, but he never asks if Jack's in.'

'Oh, Madge! have you borne this all this

time and never let us know? How could you go on bearing it alone? If we had known—if I had known, nothing should have kept me away.'

'You could not have done anything, darling, if you had been here. I think papa was glad for Adela—for you to be away, for no one to see the shame and misery that has come upon us but ourselves. Hush! there's the latch.'

But it wasn't the latch; it was only the wind playing strange pranks round the kitchen door, hurling itself against it, and rattling the old latch as if it were an evil spirit striving to come in.

Nestling close to each other, the two watchers sat through the small hours of the night, and still Jack did not come. The wind howled round the corner of the house, and above the great chimney where they sat, and where the snow, mixed with soot, fell down in great hissing blobs into the fire, but the latch was not lifted. A feeble cricket was chirping under the hearth, and now and again a mouse would scurry across the floor out of some cranny in the old warped panelling, and the old clock in the hall, ticking loud in the still house, seemed like some familiar voice speaking from the long-dead past—the dead happy past.

'Has he ever been as late as this before?' Molly asked fearfully, as the clock warned solemnly for the striking of another hour.

'Yes, dearie. Don't tremble so—he is often later than this.'

'And you have sat up alone! Oh, Madge! how could you?'

The clock was true to its warning; one by one it beat out the solemn strokes of the hour. As the last stroke went echoing drearily through the silent house the latch was lifted and Jack came in.

If, indeed, it were Jack! A wild, unkempt figure, besotted and reeling, with bloodshot eyes and incoherent tongue. Molly had never seen anyone drunk in her life, and she shrank from him in terror and clung to her sister. He staggered across the floor, and would have fallen among the embers if Madge hadn't put out her arms to catch him and led him to a seat.

'You mustn't make a noise,' she said firmly, 'and you must take off your shoes. You must not go upstairs in those thick shoes, or papa will hear.'

'N--o—o—o,' he said thickly, 'never—do—wake—poor—ole—man. Poor—ole—man!'

And then he laughed a dreadful, mirthless laugh that sent a shiver through the trembling girls.

'You mustn't make a noise. You must not do that again, Jack. Remember papa!'

'Remember—papa. How—can—I—help—remembering—papa?' he hiccoughed; and then he began to whimper in a miserable, maudlin manner that quite froze Molly's blood.

Oh, it was horrible!

'Poor papa! Poor ole man!'

While Molly was trembling and powerless, Madge was kneeling down before her brother and taking off his heavy shoes, which were covered with snow. She got them off at last, and took him over to the stairs that the servants used, which were at the other side of the kitchen, and Molly heard her guiding his uncertain footsteps up the back-stairs, and he was whimpering all the way, 'Poor ole man! Poor—ole—man!'

## CHAPTER XXXV.

### THAT LITTLE BILL.

'We were rusticated, plucked, in disgrace and debt, and chucked,
Out of patience were our friends—and unkind.'

THE quiet, sad days stole on. The two sisters clung more closely to each other in their trouble, hiding as well as they might from other members of the household the misdoings of their unhappy brother.

Molly had told Madge the mysterious hints that Jack had dropped of a deeper disgrace that awaited them, and an indistinct dread of something vague and terrible was ever present in their minds. This fear gathered strength, if it didn't assume any tangible form, daily, and the trembling, bewildered girls looked helplessly in each other's faces, and shrank from any attempt to define their fears.

A letter came for Jack one morning, a cold miserable January morning when they were having breakfast. The Rector opened the letter-bag and passed the letter across to Madge. Molly saw him take it out of the bag, and look at it with some suspicion, and she noticed that his hand trembled as he passed it across the table.

It was addressed in an aristocratic female hand, and there was a crest in black on the seal. The letter was evidently from a lady.

Molly was in the old schoolroom when Jack opened it. He came down to breakfast with a furious headache, as usual. There were no small sodas on the table, no brandy in the schoolroom cupboard; there was nothing ready to alleviate his suffering or drown his care.

There was the teapot on the table, and a kettle simmering on the hob, and some dry toast that Molly had just made.

They waited upon him, in spite of his folly, as if he had been the best of brothers, and covered up all his misdoings. Not all women have a touch of the angel in them, but surely some have.

The angel in Molly got very angry sometimes; it was angry now, and it was curious. It was dying to know who that letter was from.

Jack took up the letter with a sudden flush of colour rising up beneath his sallow skin, and he opened it eagerly.

Molly watched him read it, and she saw the colour flame up into his face, and die as suddenly away and leave it quite livid. He ground his heel into the worn schoolroom hearthrug, and rapped out an oath as he crushed the letter up in his hand.

He would have thrown it in the fire, but he saw Molly standing there, by the mantelpiece, and he changed his mind and put it in his pocket.

She dared not ask him who the letter was from; all her old spirit had gone out of her: the daily spectacle of this miserable wreck had quite unnerved her. She made the tea, scalding her hand in doing it, and put it on the table before him, but he did not seem to notice it.

'Why don't you take your breakfast, Jack? it will be dinner-time presently,' she said rather bitterly.

Jack's only reply was to swear ungraciously at the dinner, and push the unoffending little black teapot impatiently away from him, and it took offence at the unusual treatment, and rolled over and fell with a crash on the floor.

'Good gracious! it will run down into papa's study,' Molly exclaimed, as she saw the brown scalding liquid making as fast as it could for the gaping cracks between the boards of the schoolroom floor.

She had to seize the first thing that came to hand to wipe it up, a little rag of a knitted thing that was no good at all. Then she tore off her apron, and knelt down on the floor dabbing away at the scalding flood.

'Papa's study!' Jack repeated. 'I'm awfully sorry it's over papa's study. Try this;' and he took out a big silk handkerchief from his pocket and threw it down to Molly.

'Poor papa! poor old man!' she heard him saying to himself as he crossed the room and went out, leaving his breakfast untasted. While she was still on the floor wiping it up, and gathering up the tea-leaves and the broken pieces of the teapot, she heard him descending the back-stairs, and the door that led out into the yard close behind him.

When she got up from the floor, and shook

her skirts out, the letter that Jack had just read lay at her feet. He had pulled it out with his pocket-handkerchief.

Molly picked up the letter with a guilty feeling, as if she had come by it in some dishonourable way, and then, with her heart throbbing, and her colour coming and going, she went off to find Madge.

Here, then, was the secret of Jack's trouble. She was quite sure that it had something to do with the impending trouble he so much dreaded, she told Madge, as they stood turning the letter over and questioning whether they were justified in reading it.

'If you think that,' said the elder sister decisively, 'I should not hesitate to read it. We may be able to help him, if we only know how. God knows we are his truest friends, and would do anything in the world to save him!'

The girls read it together, but they could not make much of it.

It was from Mr. Brackenbury's mother, and dated from Cannes.

'DEAR SIR' (it began),
'Seeing your letter to my son, marked *Immediate*, I ventured to open it. I am both surprised and grieved at the contents. In June last my son wrote me that he was in great trouble to raise a sum of money to pay a very urgent debt. I could not send him the money. I had not got it to send. But I sent him some valuable old family rings. I took them off my fingers to send them, and I understood the debt was paid.

'I am sorry I cannot help you about the bill you refer to as being a mutual obligation. I am deeply sorry if my son has held out any promise of assistance and has failed to keep it. I fear you must not rely upon him. I cannot tell you where a letter will find him.

He left me, in some misunderstanding, at Christmas, and the last time I heard of him he was at Rome.

'With my deepest regrets,
 'I am, sincerely yours,
  'JULIA BRACKENBURY.'

'Who is her son, and what has he to do with Jack?' Madge asked.

'A great deal, I fear,' said Molly, wringing her hands. 'Jack calls him, and I think with reason, "that devil Brackenbury."'

She was thinking of that night on the Granta, when Mr. Brackenbury reluctantly drew her out of the dark water and left her shivering on the bank. She was thinking also of Dorothy Piggott.

'And what about this bill?'

'The bill? It's some wickedness—some devilry of Mr. Brackenbury's. He could turn Jack round his finger. I wonder how much the bill is for. I wonder whether we could pay it, Madge?'

All that day the girls were revolving in their minds plans for raising money. Molly hadn't any trinkets to speak of—a bead necklace, a few silver bangles, a garnet ring. A pawnbroker would have turned up his nose at the lot.

There were some trinkets that had once belonged to their mother that were in Madge's keeping. Should they part with those for the salvation of her son—if, indeed, they would save him? Molly was ready to give up her share, and Madge was more than willing; but would Adela consent to it?

They put it to her during the day. They had an indefinite feeling that if anything was to be done it was to be done quickly. They did not tell her what they had learned. They only put a case before her. They suggested that Jack might be pressed for debts he had contracted which he feared coming to his father's ears. They surmised that it was this dreadful weight that was pressing him down —that was driving him into intemperance to drown remorse, and the ever-present dread of impending ruin.

Adela heard them very calmly, and pushed aside her Greek author to give their communication all her attention.

'And what do you propose to do?' she asked. 'I don't see that we can interfere.'

Only Madge had the courage to speak.

'We propose finding out what this debt is that is dragging Jack down,' she said—'that is ruining his life and spoiling all his future— and—and we are going to try to pay it.'

'We? Who? And how are you going to pay it? I'm sure I haven't any money to spare.'

'We none of us have any money to spare,' said Madge abjectly. 'We—Molly and I—

proposed to—to sell the few family jewels we have, that are in my care, that belonged to our dear mother. I am sure, looking down from her high place, she would approve of it. If it will save Jack, I—I am sure it would be right.'

Adela was speechless, but her colour came and went, and her eyes spoke volumes.

'It is only for you to consent,' Madge continued. 'It has nothing to do with papa.'

'It has everything to do with papa,' said Adela, when she had recovered her breath. 'I shall go to him at once, and tell him of this mad project. You are not fit to be trusted with the jewels, Madge, if you are led away like this! It is one of Molly's quixotic schemes, I expect. Sell mamma's jewels to pay Jack's college debts. It's perfectly monstrous!'

There was nothing more to be said, and

the girls turned sorrowfully away ; but Molly was never nearer pinching Adela in her life.

Jack was later than ever that night. He had gone out so hurriedly in the morning that he had forgotten to take Peter, and the little faithful dumb brute sat watching beside the kitchen door, now and again breaking out into a low wail, which the girls, who were huddled up in the chimney corner, were afraid every minute their father would hear.

But the old Rector slept on ; or, if he didn't sleep, he made no sign, and towards morning Jack came in.

Peter followed his master up the backstairs, and Jack, who took no notice of the girls, hiccoughed a maudlin greeting to him as he followed closely at his heels, giving vent to his joy in little sharp barks that sent awful terrors through the girls.

'Poor—ole—Peter ! Poor—ole—man !

Poor—ole—man !' they heard Jack murmuring up the stairs.

The next day an awful event happened. A man drove over to the Rectory soon after breakfast and inquired for the Rector. He was shown by the servant into the study, and Madge only caught a glimpse of him as he was going in at the door.

She didn't like the glimpse she caught.

'It is an iron-gray man in an iron-gray coat,' she said to Molly, 'and—and I think he has come about that trouble of Jack's.'

The Rector came out of the study presently with a face ashen pale, and beads of perspiration standing out on his forehead.

'Where is Jack ?' he asked hoarsely.

'He is not up yet, papa,' said Madge gently.

'Not up ?  Tell him to come down at once. Tell him to come to me in the study at once.'

Madge tremblingly obeyed. Had the sword really fallen ?

Jack was not long in obeying the summons. He came down into the room where the girls were with a wild, hunted look in his poor soddened face that went to their hearts. He had dressed hurriedly, and he had no collar or necktie on, and his hair was dishevelled, and he wore a beard of several days' growth.

'Papa,' he said ; ' does he want me ?'

There was an awful eagerness in his voice.

The Rector heard him, and came across the passage from his study into the dining-room, and shut the door. He had a paper in his hand—a blue paper with a stamp upon it.

'Do you know anything about this ?' he said sternly, holding the paper open before Jack.

Jack's poor pale soddened face grew livid,

and his voice was husky and ashamed in his throat.

'Yes, father,' he said; 'I did it.'

'You?' gasped the Rector; 'you?'

'Yes, father. God knows I did it without any intention of wrong. I was told that— that you would not be answerable.'

'You forged my name!' said the Rector, and his voice was hoarse with passion. 'You deliberately copied my signature to a bill you had no means to pay? Oh, God! that I should have a son who is a swindler and a forger!'

'No, no! not that, father—anything but that! The bill was not all mine; it was another man's. He promised to meet it. He told me that your name would never appear in it—that it was only a matter of form. I will swear it on my oath, father!'

Jack's face was horribly agitated, and

shining wet with perspiration. It was dreadful to see a man so moved.

'I will not believe you on your oath. I will not take the word of a forger and a swindler. Henceforth you are no son of mine; I renounce you from this moment! I give you up! Get out of this house, and never, never darken my doors again!'

Jack reeled like one stunned, and the girls thought he would have fallen.

A wild prayer rose in Molly's heart that he might fall there and die at the old man's feet.

'Do you hear?' continued the Rector in his harsh, strident tones, that cut the trembling wretch before him to the heart like a knife. 'Do you hear what I say? Leave this house!'

'Do you mean it, father?' said Jack huskily.

'Mean it? I call Heaven to witness that

I mean it! Get you gone, swindler! forger!'

'God forgive you, father,' said Jack in a broken voice. 'I am very sorry. Remember always—*I am—very—sorry.*'

The old man went out and left Jack standing there beside the table in his own accustomed place — the place he had lost — where he had sat in his high chair in the old childish days; where he had knelt when his baby hands could scarce reach the table, where his lips in childhood, in youth, in manhood, had repeated the old familiar words day after day, year after year, until they were burnt into his brain, and he had begun to think there was some meaning in them: 'Forgive us our trespasses, as we forgive them that trespass against us.'

Perhaps some remembrance of those old days came to him in that supreme moment, as he stood there a discarded outcast from his father's roof; perhaps some echo of those oft-repeated words mingled with the tumult in his brain.

Surely he had missed their meaning.

The two girls, who were mute spectators of the miserable scene, clung to each other in an agony of silence. What could they say?

Madge, looking across the table at him, saw through her tears, not the stricken prodigal, with his ashen face and trembling limbs, but the frank, bright-faced boy his mother had committed to her care with her dying breath. She didn't think of him in his shame; she thought of his mother in her high happy place.

Oh, if she could see him now!

Jack's eyes followed the old man to the door of the room with a hungry, yearning entreaty in them like some hunted creature driven to bay; and then he pulled himself together and went slowly up the stairs, stumbling forward like one in a dream.

'Oh, Jack, what are you going to do?' sobbed Molly. She broke away from Madge's clinging arms and followed him upstairs.

He did not answer her until he reached the door of his own room.

'Do?' he said. 'There is but one thing for me to do. Go—go. God knows where! It doesn't matter where. I must pack up a few things, Molly, and then I'll go.'

'Oh, Jack, you mustn't go! Indeed, indeed, papa did not mean it. He spoke hastily. You know you have tried him a good deal lately; and he spoke in anger. He will think better of it presently. Oh! indeed you mustn't go!'

Molly was clinging to him, and her tears were falling fast. He disengaged her clinging arms gently.

'Yes,' he said huskily, and with a sob in

his throat; 'it's all over, Molly; it's all over, my dear. It's very good of you to be so awfully sorry for me. I don't deserve it, but I must go, all the same. Forger and swindler! Good God! Molly, I couldn't stay another hour in the house. Get me a little bag, dear, something to put my things in, and let me go.'

He would not be persuaded, and Molly reluctantly brought a bag, and stood with streaming eyes in the doorway watching him throw a few necessary things in, while Peter, after a few suspicious sniffs, began to whine and made frantic efforts to lick his hand.

'Have you got any money, Jack?' Molly asked.

'No,' he said; 'I was cleaned out long ago. I've left a score behind me at the Golden Lion. I dare say the landlord there would let me have a sovereign if—if I gave him my watch.'

He pulled out of his pocket as he spoke an old-fashioned silver lever watch.

'Father gave me it when I first went up,' he said, 'and it's a capital watch. I think he'd square off the account and give me a pound besides ;' and he returned the watch to his waistcoat-pocket with a sigh.

Molly ran out of the room, and she turned out her desk. There was very little money in it. She had spent all the money she had saved in buying pretty things for the house in Cambridge, and gyps and bedmakers were decorating their best parlours with them now.

There were a few gold coins she had hoarded up for some special articles in her trousseau—it was all she had in the world—and she brought it humbly to Jack.

'It is all I have, dear,' she said, pressing it humbly upon him. 'I wish it were more, but it will keep you from leaving your watch—the watch poor papa gave you—at the Golden Lion. Never mind about the debt there, Jack. We will pay it—Madge and I will pay it. Oh, Jack, must you go ?'

The brother and sister were in the old schoolroom when Madge joined them. Jack had on his overcoat, and his bag and stick in his hand, and Peter was whining at his heels. He was such a limp, dejected Peter ; he had scented trouble in the air ; he hadn't spirit enough to wag his tail.

Madge's eyes were red with weeping, and her face was very grave and sad. She had just come from her father. She had been pleading with him for Jack, but the Rector was inexorable.

Jack had sinned beyond pardon. He had incurred a debt of five hundred pounds, and he had forged his father's signature to a bill. He should not stay another hour beneath his roof ; he should go away at once—an outcast and a stranger—to return no more.

Madge's sorrowful face told how unavailing had been her intercession.

'It's awfully good of you girls to take so much trouble about me,' said Jack, moved in spite of himself. 'I'm afraid I've not deserved it of you. I've been behaving like a beast. I hope you'll forgive me, girls!'

The tears were in his eyes, and his voice was broken. The sisters clung to him, and would have held him back, but he kissed them and broke away from them.

'Oh, Jack! my own dear, dear boy! You *will* write?' sobbed Madge. She was fumbling at his waistcoat-pocket, and Molly caught sight of a familiar little netted purse she was trying to stuff in without Jack seeing it. 'Promise me you will write?'

'I can't promise, Madge. It will be better not. I shall go abroad, I hope. If I ever do any good you will hear of it soon enough. If—if I fail—if I go to the dogs, it is better for you not to know. God bless you, girls—and reward you ! Take care of the dear old pater. Poor old man !'

He broke away from them, and went down the stairs with the old cry on his lips—' Poor old man !'

The girls watched him from the schoolroom window going down the road—a black drooping figure in the white landscape, with Peter following at his heels.

It was sadder than a funeral.

# CHAPTER XXXVI.

### DARK DAYS.

There was a long spell of cold dreary weather after Jack went away.

But the blight and the chill that lay upon the beautiful green world outside the Rectory windows was nothing to the chilling atmosphere within.

The Rector never spoke of his prodigal son after that awful day. He paid the debt that Jack had incurred without Mr. Brackenbury's assistance. He had to sell the college rick, and Brindle—the dun cow—and her calf; and the 'old lady' and her family went, too.

He had to get the money how he could.

However, he got it, the bill was paid, and the nasty bit of blue stamped paper, with that fine copy of his signature upon it—that Jack had unwillingly made on that morning—was in his possession.

Nobody but Molly and Madge ever knew the right of that sad story. Adela never heard the truth—the naked truth. She knew that Jack had gone away ; that his father had discarded him—had driven him out of the house like a dog. She didn't know why, and she didn't ask why. She never had any faith in Jack.

He didn't even wish her good-bye. He went without a sign, and left her—the sister he had played with, and quarrelled with, all his life, poring over her Greek author in her own cosy sanctum.

She didn't know that he had gone till she came down to dinner, and saw the girls' tear-stained faces.

She had no patience with them, crying for Jack. For her own part, she thought it served him right.

'I am not at all sorry papa has found him out,' she said sweetly. 'He always thought a great deal too much of him.'

She went back to Cambridge a few days after, and the girls were not sorry when she went. Molly wept a little when she had gone; she was thinking of the old time when they went together, and Jack was with them. She was getting used to tears now. It seemed to her that her cup had brimmed over too soon, and that there was nothing left but the bitter lees to drain. All her best hopes had slipped away from her.

After Adela had gone, Madge—quiet, patient, uncomplaining Madge—fell ill. The anxiety and sorrow of the last few weeks told upon her, and her health broke down under it.

She had grown suddenly old and gray and

worn-looking, and she had a nasty cough. The doctor ordered her to keep indoors, and prescribed a tonic.

Madge yielded, and took the tonic he sent her submissively. She had no heart to go out of doors and face the inquiries of all the old cronies in the village, of what had become of 'Master Jack.'

Molly took her place in the parish. She was glad to have something to do. And then a very unexpected change came over her. Instead of being sick and impatient, as she used to be, when the old women entered into minute and wearisome details of their unpleasant complaints, she found herself, much to her own surprise, being sorry for them. She bore with the old men, too, and listened to their rambling talk : their reminiscences of the days before she was born ; their stories of the sons and daughters they had brought up —the girls who had married and gone away, the boys who had gone to foreign parts. Her eyes often grew dim listening to the simple and touching annals of the poor.

She had no idea until now that rich and poor were all made of the same clay; that the hammer of sorrow beat them all into pretty much the same shape.

There were some homes in the village she could not trust herself to go into. Happy homes mostly. She told herself that she was not needed there, but she looked with a strange yearning in her eyes through the open doors, or the uncurtained windows in the firelight, and saw the young mothers with the little children round their knees and infants in their arms.

Molly would turn away from such sights with a dumb cry of anguish in her heart. She didn't know, until she looked through those cottage windows in the winter nights, what she had missed in life. She never knew until she had lost him how much she loved the Junior Dean.

Adela had only mentioned him once in her letters since her return. 'He has not come up this term,' she said, and it was rumoured that he had resigned his fellowship.

And this was all that Molly heard of her old lover for many weary months. She began, like Madge, to search the pages of the *Record*, but she never met with a scrap of information about him.

There was nothing more heard about Jack —not a word, not a sign—whether he were living or dead. The brave, gallant young life that had started with such splendid promise had shrivelled up suddenly. There was only the black shadow of undying remembrance hanging over the unhappy household.

With the wet, windy spring days came a

new care to the sisters. Their father's health began to give way. The bitter trials that had come to him had sunk deeper into his heart by reason of the silent stoicism of his endurance.

He never complained. He went about his work just as usual, taking the two services on Sundays, and teaching in the schools, and spending the hours of the day, when he was not shut up in his study, in visiting in the parish. He would return in the chilly dusk, after a long walk over wet fields and wetter Devonshire lanes, that led to distant farms and cottages in that widely-scattered parish, looking wretchedly ill and worn out; but he never admitted that he was ill—only tired. He got tired sooner now, the girls remarked, than he used to.

His hair had grown quite gray soon after Jack went away, and his eyes were sunk deeper than ever beneath his shaggy eyebrows, and his big cheek-bones were unusually prominent.

The girls talked about his altered looks between themselves ; but they hadn't the courage to broach the subject to him.

'You look a little tired, papa,' Molly had ventured to say one day, when he came in after a longer round of visiting than usual.

'Yes,' he said, with a sigh ; 'I am tired. I shall not go there again. Has the postman been ?'

It was quite late in the afternoon, and the postman always came in the morning, during breakfast, so that Molly looked up in astonishment when her father asked the question.

There was a strange look on his face that she had never seen there before—a dreamy, bewildered look that startled her.

'Yes, papa,' she answered, in a tone of surprise. 'He came this morning, as usual.'

'This morning ?' the Rector repeated, passing his hand across his forehead with a puzzled air, as if trying to collect his thoughts —'this morning? I don't remember his coming. Was there no letter from Jack?'

It was the first time he had mentioned his son's name since that dreadful day, and Molly was so frightened that she could scarcely keep herself from crying out.

'No, papa,' she faltered; 'there was no letter. There has been no letter since—since he went away.'

'No,' said the Rector; 'it is very careless of him. He ought to write.'

He got up from the chair by the fire and went out of the room repeating the words, 'He ought to write,' and that dreamy, bewildered look was still in his eyes.

He went straight over to his study and shut the door, and Molly flew upstairs to tell Madge what a strange thing had happened.

Madge was not at all frightened.

'Papa has always been forgetful,' she said, 'and this anxiety has told upon his nerves, and these long walks in the wind and rain are too much for him.'

There was nothing more said about Jack till the following morning, when the letter-bag was opened. Her father's hand shook so, Molly noticed, that he could hardly turn the key. He tossed the contents over impatiently, and laid the few letters and papers the post had brought down by the side of his plate.

'There is no letter from Jack,' he said, in a tone of disappointment, and he looked across the table to his elder daughter, who was pouring out the tea, with a pained look on his face.

'Did you expect one, papa?' she asked, startled out of herself by the words and the look that accompanied them.

'Yes,' he said thoughtfully; 'he ought to

have written before now. How long is it since he went back?'

'He has been gone three weeks, papa,' said Molly, with a little wail in her voice, and her eyes filled with tears.

'Three weeks!' he repeated—'surely not three weeks?' and then there came a dazed look into his eyes—a sort of dreamy wonder and confusion—and he set down the cup he held in his shaking hand, untasted.

The girls were silent, and looked at each other across the table.

'I think you are wrong, my dear, in the date,' he said irritably. 'I will look at the almanack and see. It cannot be three weeks.'

He got up from the table and went into his study, and he did not leave it again all the morning. He did not mention the subject again at dinner-time, and after dinner he went over to the church. He had to take a funeral.

The girls watched him go down the path,

and Molly fancied that his walk was altered. It was not the old firm, manly step—rather a long step to keep up with—but a short, weak, shambling step, and one foot seemed to drag after him.

She remarked it to Madge as they stood watching the little black procession file into the churchyard.

'Nonsense,' said Madge the practical; 'papa is walking exactly the same as usual. It is one of his old attacks of forgetfulness. He will remember everything presently. I wish *I* could forget sometimes;' and the tears came into her eyes.

It was a bitterly cold day, and the wind was blowing unspeakably in that exposed churchyard, where he stood with his uncovered head in the rain and sleet.

He seemed to have changed visibly when he came back to the Rectory after the funeral. His figure was stooping and shrunken, and his cheek-bones and his knees were more prominent than ever, and there was a painful look upon his face.

'The post has not come in?' he said, looking from one to the other.

'No, papa; it came in this morning. Don't you remember?' said Madge.

'Yes, yes, to be sure; and there was no letter from Jack?'

'No, papa, there was no letter from Jack.'

He fell asleep over his tea, and woke up with a little start and a smile on his face—the first smile they had seen since Jack had come back in disgrace.

'Lucky I kept the glebe in hand,' he said, looking over to Madge with his feeble smile; 'it will be a capital shear this year. The college rick will be larger than ever.'

'I am quite sure he's not fit to preach to-morrow,' said Molly. 'I'm quite sure he ought to have a doctor.'

But he did preach the next day, which happened to be Sunday. When Madge ventured to suggest that he was not looking well, and that he ought to consult a doctor, the Rector got very angry. He was quite well, he said ; he had never felt better. The cold wind in the churchyard had tried him ; that was all. There was nothing the matter with him.

There was no post on Sunday mornings at Silverton, and for the first time in her life Molly was quite grateful for it. She would not have gone through that dreadful scene of the previous morning, when her father searched in vain for a letter from Jack, for the world.

He was looking much as usual the next morning when he came down to breakfast. He was looking much as usual when he went over to the church, and he walked with his old firm step, and his head erect.

He went through the service as usual ; and he went up into the pulpit and looked round the church, and down upon the old familiar faces in the pews below. He must have known every one of his flock penned up here, as a shepherd knows the faces of his sheep. It seemed to Molly that he was looking round for someone.

Still with that anxious look in his eyes he read out the text : 'For this my son was dead, and is alive again ; he was lost, and is found.'

Everybody in the church opened their eyes and pricked up their ears, however that operation may be performed. At any rate, they listened attentively. Surely they should hear something now of the trouble that everyone in the village knew had been hanging over the Rectory — something of that unhappy difference which had arisen between father and son.

The Rector paused after he had delivered his text, and looked round the church until his eye rested upon the Rectory pew, where Jack had been used to sit all his life; and then he smiled and began his sermon.

He spoke slowly and impressively, dwelling on the frailty and infirmity of human nature, and the necessity, the divine necessity, of forgiveness; the yearning love of the father's heart over the returning prodigal, the love that saw him while yet a great way off, and had compassion on him, and ran to meet him, and fell on his neck, and kissed him.

'Oh, how could he preach such words?' the girls asked themselves. The tears were running down their faces, and their hearts were throbbing with agony.

That miserable scene when Jack was driven like a dog from the home of his childhood was before their eyes, and his cry, his bitter cry, 'Father, I am sorry!' was in their ears.

And still the old man went on preaching. There was a hectic flush on his cheeks, and his eyes were unnaturally bright, and his lips were moving rapidly. He was describing in tender, touching words the mutual joy of the forgiver and the forgiven.

'There was nothing,' he went on to say. 'that the father's heart of love could deny to the repentant child: the best robe, the ring for his defiled hands, the shoes for his weary, wandering feet—beauty for ashes; love, exceeding love, for condemnation and despair.'

'Oh, how could he preach such words?'

There was not a dry eye in the church, and Madge, the quiet, self-possessed Madge, was sobbing audibly; but Molly was watching her father.

He paused in the middle of a sentence, and looked over to the Rectory pew, and when he saw only the two girls there, he turned away with a pained, bewildered look on his face. as if he had expected to see somebody else there, and was disappointed.

He could not pick up the thread of his sermon again. He attempted to speak once or twice, but his lips gave forth no sound, and he looked helplessly around with that strange, bewildered look in his eyes, and there was a painful silence. Had he forgotten his sermon ?

The interval was so long that the congregation began to be alarmed, and looked anxiously over at the Rector's daughters in the big square Rectory pew.

Molly didn't see the looks of alarm that were directed to them ; her eyes were fixed on her father with a dreadful, unspeakable terror in her mind.

His eyes were wandering helplessly round the church with a wild, cloudy look in them she had never seen in any eyes before—a sort of dreamy bewilderment, as if he were suddenly loosed from his moorings in life, and were drifting out into an unknown sea.

Even while she looked his face changed. His eyes had travelled slowly round the church, resting on every familiar face with a strangely solemn look, until they rested on the family pew where his children sat. But he didn't see them. He was not looking for them. Whatever he saw, it altered the fashion of his countenance: perhaps it was the face of the wife he had lost so many years ago; perhaps it was the face of the son he had driven forth an outcast but yesterday —not the wild, tear-stained face of the prodigal, but the fresh, bright, boyish face that used to look over the top of the Rectory pew.

The wan wintry sunshine flickered in through the high windows, and lighted up that corner where Jack used to stand on a seat when a little child, with his long fair curls falling over the quaint old carvings on the front of the pew.

Perhaps the old Rector saw them now, for the bewilderment went out of his face, and he smiled, and raised his hands slowly in benediction—and fell heavily forward.

# CHAPTER XXXVII.

'O ABSALOM, MY SON, MY SON!'

THEY carried the old Rector to his bed and sent for medical aid.

He was unconscious for many days, and when he again opened his eyes upon the world that was slowly receding from him, his mind was a blank.

No, not a blank. Only the present, and things relating to the present, were a blank. The past was fresh and green; only the past lived in his memory. Paralysis of the brain had mercifully blotted out every remembrance of disappointment and pain and sorrow and loss.

He was back again in these last days with the wife of his youth ; and his children were again about his knee. He used to take Molly for the mother she could scarcely remember, as she sat in his room nursing him through those sad winter days.

'Don't you know me, papa?' she cried, trembling all over, the first time he addressed her as his long-lost wife.

'Know you, Mary? Of course I know you. Oh, my darling, I am so glad you have come back ! You have been away so long !'

There were the services at the church to think about, and the parish to see to, and everything devolved upon Madge.

She wrote at once, when the doctor told her how hopeless her father's condition was, to the Rector of a neighbouring parish, begging him to send her someone to take her father's place the following Sunday, while she looked out for a curate.

She advertised in the *Guardian* and the *Record* for a curate to come immediately, but her advertisement did not appear in time for any replies to reach her until too late for the forthcoming Sunday.

The anxiety about her father, and the church, and all the worry and trouble of that dreadful winter, had told upon Madge, and when that miserable Sunday morning came she was looking like a ghost of her former self.

The neighbouring Rector had sent a messenger over only the previous night to say that a friend staying with him on a visit had offered to take the services on the morrow, and all this time Madge had been kept in dreadful anxiety and suspense.

She had sat up with her father half the night, and was looking so utterly worn out and wretched, when church time came, that she decided she would stay at home, and that

Molly should go in her place, and bring the stranger back to dinner.

Molly went to church and sat in the Rectory pew alone; but she did not bring the stranger back to dinner. She was so weighed down with the remembrance of what had happened only the previous Sunday that she took very little notice of the stranger who filled her father's place. She sat weeping quietly in the shelter of that high old-fashioned pew through the prayers without once looking up. The prayers and the Litany sounded differently this morning, perhaps because they were read by a different voice. Every familiar entreaty for strength, and mercy, and deliverance sounded so differently now. She had repeated them thousands of times before — they dropped nimbly off her tongue; but to-day they sank into her heart fraught with quite a new meaning.

Perhaps she had never needed mercy and strength before. The happy ask for these things daily as well as the sorrowful; but they don't want them; unfortunately, there are only one set of prayers for all.

The first time she looked up through the service was at the beginning of the sermon, when an unfamiliar voice gave out the text; and then, instead of looking at his congregation, the new preacher was looking at her. Whenever she looked up during the sermon the preacher was looking over to the Rectory pew.

There wasn't much to see there, only a girl with a red nose and eyes swollen with weeping.

She waited for him in the porch, but he would not come over to the Rectory to dinner. He was going to dine with some friends in the village, he said, and after making some kind inquiries after her father, he hurried away across the wet fields, and left her standing by herself in the porch.

He was a commonplace-looking man, with a shy, nervous manner, and the smile with which he greeted Molly in the porch when he found her waiting for him died out suddenly directly she spoke to him. She went back feeling dreadfully afraid that her invitation had been cold and formal, and that Madge would rate her soundly for not bringing him back to dinner.

Madge wasn't at all sorry. It was a relief to her that he had found a friend in the village, and that she hadn't got to entertain a stranger with that racking headache. Her father had been unusually restless all the morning. He had been calling for his dead wife, and would not be pacified.

'Dear mamma is in heaven,' said Madge, weeping in spite of herself at his repeated entreaties for her to come to his bedside.

'In heaven! She is here. She was here not a minute ago. She was sitting where you are, and she had Jack in her arms.'

He had fallen into a light sleep when Molly came back from church, and she did not go into his room again until after dinner; and then, when Madge went upstairs to get ready for church, she went in.

The curtains were drawn so as to shade his eyes from the light, and he did not notice her entrance until she was standing beside his bed. He gave a cry, and lifted his head eagerly from the pillow, and a great light came into his face.

'Oh, Mary!' he cried; 'have you come at last? I have been waiting for you so long! You must not leave me again.'

'No, papa; I will not leave you. I have come to sit with you all the afternoon while the rest go to church.'

All the rest went to church, Madge and

the two servants ; and Molly was left alone in the house. It did not occur to her to be afraid until they had gone—until she heard the door shut, and she caught sight of their receding figures disappearing into the church.

Then for the first time she noticed that her father was more restless than usual, and that his cheek was flushed and his eyes brighter than she had seen them since his illness.

'Where is Jack ?' he asked presently.

'Jack, papa ? He—he is gone away.'

'Gone back to Cambridge ? Yes, yes, of course he has. But he was here just now. He was sitting where you are. I don't think he is gone back. Will you go and see, my dear ?'

He was so persistent that Molly had to go out of the room, to the head of the stairs, on an ineffectual search for Jack. When she came back he was watching the door with a wistful look in his eyes.

'Have you found him?' he asked eagerly. 'Is he coming?'

'No, papa; I haven't found him. He has really gone,' she said sadly.

He sank back on his pillow with a sigh, and his face clouded. But it was only for a minute, when he turned sharply to her again with the old question:

'Where is Jack?'

It was no use to tell him that Jack had gone away. He was quite sure that Jack was in the house.

And so the wet, windy afternoon wore on, and Molly soothed and pacified her father as best she could, going out on the landing so many times on that fruitless errand to search for Jack, and coming back to find him watching eagerly, with that expectant look on his face and the old question on his lips:

'Where's Jack?'

He grew restless at last, and made an effort to get out of bed and 'look for Jack himself.'

'He is downstairs,' he said. 'I hear him talking. I am not so deaf that I shouldn't know my son's voice and his footstep. I couldn't mistake his footstep; I've listened for it too many years not to know it. Firm and strong, with a spring in it there is in no other. I couldn't mistake it. There! I hear it now, in the room below. I must needs go and find him, if he won't come to me.'

The old man threw off the bedclothes and began to dress. It was no use Molly trying to keep him in bed. He would not be held back. His strength had come back, and he pushed her aside, with that sudden fierce energy that had come to him, like a reed.

She gave him the clothes he insisted upon putting on, even helping him with her trembling hands to dress, listening meanwhile with straining ears for the sound of footsteps on the gravel beneath.

'Would they never come back from church?' she asked herself, as she wrung her hands unavailingly when the old man insisted on going over the house to look for Jack.

Though he was possessed with this fierce, sudden strength that enabled him to dress, when he reached the staircase he staggered to and fro like a drunken man, and would have fallen if Molly had not thrown her arms around him and held him up.

The paroxysm was passing, and he feebly clutched at the banisters for support.

How eagerly Molly listened for approaching footsteps! Would they never come?

She couldn't get him away from the stairs, and every moment she feared he would fall. It would be death to him in his feeble state to fall down those stairs, and how could she support him till help came?

'Oh, papa, if you would go back to your room,' she pleaded, 'Jack will come to you. If he is in the house, I am sure he will come to you. He isn't downstairs, papa; indeed he isn't downstairs.'

'You have not called him. How should you know? Call him, my dear.'

'Jack! Jack!' Molly called down over the stairs, and a mocking echo went travelling through all the deserted rooms of the silent house.

'You don't call loud enough, my dear.' said the old man. 'Let me call. He will hear me. He will know my voice wherever he is. Jack! my dear boy! where are you? Jack! Jack!'

The feeble, querulous voice rang through the house in its pathetic entreaty; but there was no response—only the weak, tremulous echo wailing through the passages.

'He is not downstairs. papa,' said Molly, 'or he would come—I am sure he would come.'

'Yes; Jack always came when I called. He was always a dutiful son, my dear. You don't know, Mary, you have been so long away. There never was a better son. He may be in his room; he hasn't got up very early lately. Let us go and see.'

The idea gave him strength, and he quite dragged Molly along the passage in the direction of Jack's room. She was glad at any cost to get him away from the stairs. If her father fell down now—and she thought he would fall every moment—he could not hurt himself like falling down over those terrible stairs.

But the Rector did not fall. He threw open the door of his son's room, and repeated his name, with an anxious, eager look on his face.

The room was just as Jack had left it. All his things were in their places. His foils and gloves against the wall; his fishing-rod over the mantelpiece; his gun in the corner; a case of butterflies he had caught when a boy hanging over his dressing-table; the skin of an otter he had killed, on the floor; his bed as he had last slept in it—nothing was changed.

His father looked round the room at all these familiar objects with a quite pathetic tenderness in his shining eyes.

'My son is not here,' he said with a sigh; 'but I will lie down on his bed. I will wait for him here.'

It was as much as Molly could do to help him over to the bed; his strength had gone as suddenly as it had come, and when he reached the bed he fell back on the pillow exhausted.

Then, and not till then, did she hear the gravel outside scrunching beneath the feet of the servants returning from church; and presently she heard Madge going upstairs.

How could she go up so blithely!

There was a spring in Madge's footsteps on

the stairs that Molly had not heard before, not for months; and she did not go to her father's room, as was her wont after a short absence in the village. She went straight to her own room and shut the door.

If Molly could have followed her sister into her room she would have been more surprised at what she saw there, than at the spring that had come so suddenly into Madge's weary footsteps.

The Rector's daughter, when she came back from church, went straight over to the glass on her dressing-table and looked in it with an eager, questioning gaze that she had never bestowed on it before.

The glass had faithfully reflected back her face in joy and sorrow for more than twenty years, and it had never deceived her once through all that time.

It did not deceive her now.

It reflected back with unwavering fidelity a

tired face, that looked prematurely old and gray and worn. It did not conceal a single line, or crow's-foot, or wrinkle. It was truthful to a fault. It did not hide from the questioning eyes that looked into it so eagerly that all the youth had gone out of the face, and the beauty too. Perhaps something better than youth and beauty had taken their place. The years must have been unkind if they had not left more than they had taken.

Madge turned away from the glass with a sigh, and then she burst into tears.

And all this time Molly was waiting by her father's side for her sister to come. She could bear it no longer, and she crept to the door of Jack's room with a pitiful cry on her lips—
'Madge! Madge!'

It sounded like the pitiful bleat of a lamb through the closed door—such a far-off, spiritless cry that Madge never recognised it for Molly's voice.

What with looking in the glass, and that little weep she had indulged in, and the subsequent bathing of her eyes it entailed, it was quite a long time before she reached her father's sick-room, and when she got there—it was empty !

The Rector refused to go back to his own room. He would stay in Jack's bed, in Jack's room, with the dear familiar signs of his recent occupation around him. He was so exhausted with the exertion he had made that it would have been difficult to move him in any case.

He scarcely moved or spoke during that sad evening when the girls watched beside his bed, taking no notice of anyone ; opening his eyes sometimes to look around the room that had once been his boy's, and smiling faintly as he closed them again.

His voice was no longer querulous. It was lower and fainter—a small, soft voice. He asked for nobody but Jack; and even when lying there, with his eyes closed, apparently asleep, he was straining his ears to listen for Jack's coming. Molly had to watch beside him through the night. If she only left the room for a moment he would miss her and inquire for her.

'Where is your mother, my dear?' he would say to Madge. 'She mustn't leave me now. It won't be for long; when my son comes I'm going away. Call your mother, my dear.'

And Madge would have to call her sister, who was trying to snatch a few hours' sleep, and the two girls watched the sick-bed together.

Towards morning there was a change—a slightly perceptible change, but both saw it at once. It might have been the flickering shadow of the night-lamp, but their father's face was changed—grayer, sharper, with a dazzled look in the faint eyes that gleamed small and bright beneath the shaggy brows drawn tight together.

Molly saw it with a strange terror at her heart. Was this death?

She had never seen death in any form, and she had seen very little sickness.

She stooped over the bed with her hand on the poor feeble fingers, that were helplessly clutching the bed-clothes. How damp they were, and cold! The contact with that poor groping hand sent quite a chill through her.

'Papa,' she said hurriedly, 'are you asleep?'

He opened his dazzled, faint eyes for a moment. 'Has Jack come?' he asked. His voice sounded faint and far-off; the sand of life was ebbing out, grain by grain. Molly was getting very much frightened, and her heart was beating dreadfully.

She drew his two clammy hands together in an attitude of prayer, and raised them between her own.

'Jack will be sure to come to you some day, papa,' she whispered; 'but will you not leave him your blessing now—your blessing and forgiveness? You would like to forgive Jack?'

The film went back from the faint eyes, and for a moment they were bright and eager.

'Forgive Jack?' he repeated; 'of course I forgive Jack. My dear boy! There is nothing that he has ever done that I do not freely forgive. God bless him! God bless my dear son!'

There was a sudden dazzled look in the shining eyes, and the last spark of consciousness died slowly out, and the film came back, and he lay looking up vacantly at the white ceiling.

'Have you no blessing for us, father?' sobbed Madge—'for your three wee girlies, as you used to call us. Have you no blessing for your girlies, father?'

The old man pressed her hand, but he gave no other sign of consciousness, and his lips were silent.

Like Israel of old, he had but one blessing.

# CHAPTER XXXVIII.

### ALONE IN THE WORLD.

It was a dreadful week after the Rector's death. But for the presence of the kind friend who had driven over on the Sunday morning to take the service, it would have been unbearable.

Fortunately, he had not left the neighbourhood, but was staying with a friend in the village. He came over the next morning and took all those sad last things into his own hands. He saved the poor crushed and broken-hearted sisters every painful detail. He took the management of everything upon himself, as if he had been one of the family.

Jack couldn't have done more than that very commonplace-looking clergyman did had he been there ; and he might possibly have done a great deal less.

He was not quite a stranger to the parish ; he had taken a temporary duty there several years ago, and many people still remembered him. Molly did not know him in the least, but Madge remembered him in a conscious, shy way that was most unusual to her. Whatever she knew of him, it gave her confidence to trust him in their sore need. The day after her father's death she told him the whole sad story of Jack's disgrace and her father's displeasure.

She did not conceal a single shameful fact; she poured out the miserable story in all its naked truth, and asked him to advise them what to do.

'Your brother should be communicated with at once,' he said, 'if he is still in

England. I remember him quite well as a bright clever boy. He was too frank and generous by nature to do any wilful wrong. If he has been led astray through these very qualities, that would be virtues in most men, we must set him right again; but the first thing to be done is to find him.'

He set about it at once. He advertised in the agony columns of the daily and weekly papers; he wrote to all the shipping agencies, he made inquiries in every quarter; but by the end of the week, the day the Rector was buried, Jack was not found.

It is so much easier to be lost than to be found.

Who can picture the anguish of those first dark days, when the Rector lay white and still in a chamber above, and the girls wept together in the darkened rooms below? Molly was more utterly crushed by this last blow than her sister.

Sorrow and loss had repeated themselves with weary iteration. They had not come to her singly, they had come in battalions.

It seemed as if the world were giving way under her feet; as if everything she loved and trusted in were slipping away from her. It was so difficult to realize that it was not all a dream, a bad dream. She went upstairs to Jack's room more than once on that first day to assure herself that her father was really there—a serene, solemn presence, not a living voice. Perhaps the serenity and the calm of the beautiful face, that death had only sculptured into a more perfect likeness of Jack, soothed her spirit more than any words of comfort and consolation.

There were very few left to whisper words of consolation to the bereaved sisters. There was the kind friend who had come so opportunely to their aid, but his ministrations were chiefly confined to Madge. Mr. Gray's brother, the tutor of Clare, came down to the funeral, but he did not bring Adela with him.

What would have been the use ? It would have interfered sadly with her work, and she could get her mourning made better in Cambridge.

Dorothy Piggott wrote a very tender little letter to Molly directly she heard of her father's death.

'Oh, my darling,' she wrote, 'I am so sorry for you ! I want to take you in my arms, and feel your wet cheek against mine, and remind you of that happy time when there will be no more crying !'

Mr. Gray stayed over the funeral and looked through his brother's papers to find a will. He found hundreds of old MS. sermons, but he found no will, no testamentary document whatever.

The loss was of no great importance, for

there was very little to bequeath. The Rector had spent all his income from year to year on the education of his children. He had kept nothing back. He had no old stocking hidden away beneath the flooring of his room, or behind the back of his bed. He had sold everything on the place—the cow and calf in the meadow, the foal in the stall, the college rick, the ' old lady ' in the stye, even the grass on the ground—to pay that debt of Jack's.

He had left nothing behind him, beside the little bag with the church collections, in the way of accumulated wealth.

There was the insurance, but that was little enough to divide among three—four, the girls said. They would not touch a penny of Jack's share. It never occurred to them, as it occurred to other people, to blame their father for having made no provision for his motherless girls. He had spent all, and more than he could afford, on their education.

He was such a hale, hearty old man, that he could have had no thought of dying. He would have been living still if Jack hadn't broken his heart.

There was a consultation held after the funeral, when the girls were feeling so utterly chilled and miserable that it did not seem to them of any importance whatever happened to them. They could not suffer more than they had suffered.

Mr. Gray was charged with a message from his wife to bring Molly back with him, but the sisters would not be separated. There was so much to be done in giving up the house, and he suggested that it should be given up at once to save expense, and there would be no one but Madge to do it.

The sisters clung to each other weeping, and begged their uncle to defer that question of the future till another day. They could not discuss it with the words of the service that had just been read over their father ringing in their ears, with that new-made grave before their eyes. They could only cling to each other and weep, and vow they would never be separated. So Mr. Gray went back to Cambridge and left the question unsettled; but he gave instructions about the sale of the furniture before he went, and communicated with the Ecclesiastical Commissioners.

The girls did not remonstrate, though this haste to break up their home and drive them out into the world appeared unseemly and cruel. They could have remained six months longer in their old home, but they must have turned out at the end of that time, and perhaps, all things considered, it was just as well to turn out now.

They began at once. It was better to begin and to take the edge off it, than to have it before their eyes, a black shadow growing gloomier and darker as the days wore on.

They began miserably and helplessly to go through the rooms and gather together the few things they would keep, and put aside the things that must be sold. All the furniture would have to be sold—the old piano, the familiar tables and chairs, the faded carpets, the pictures on the walls, the old china and little valueless ornaments that they remembered so long as they could remember anything. They could not possibly take them with them. They would have to go out into situations and earn their living like other girls. Nobody would take them in with this encumbrance. They couldn't even keep back a chest of drawers.

It was very foolish to be affected by the sight of these dumb, familiar things; but they were not dumb to the weeping girls. They were eloquent with happy memories. They were the frame, the setting, of everything that had happened to them in their lives.

While they were engaged on this miserable task, Mr. Llewelyn, the friend who had helped them in their need, was announced. He had called to take leave. He had stayed until after the funeral, and had done all that was in his power to do, and now he was going back to his own parish.

He had not been present at the family council when the future of the girls was discussed. He was not an old friend of the family; his acquaintance with their father was of the very slightest. He had only once taken a temporary charge during a summer holiday. He had no right to be present when such questions were discussed.

He had heard, however—everybody in the village had heard—that there was to be a sale, and that the girls were left almost destitute.

He looked from one to the other when he came in. He had come in so suddenly that they hadn't time to smooth the lines out of their faces, and their eyes were still wet.

'I have scarcely the right of an old friend,' he said, looking from one to the other, but his eyes rested on the elder sister; 'but my previous acquaintance, and my presence here at this time, must be my excuse for asking you if there is any way in which I can be useful to you.'

His eyes spoke so much more than his words, and his face was so earnest and sympathetic, that Molly was moved, and her tears began to flow afresh; but Mr. Llewelyn was not looking at her.

Madge flushed and her bosom swelled, but she kept the tears back.

'We are very grateful to you for what you have done for us,' she said, with a quiver in her voice, 'and for all the trouble you have taken about Jack; but for us there is nothing further to be done. We must give up this house—and go away—and—and take situations of some kind. Poor papa has been able to make but very little provision for us. We must earn our own living.'

It was not very easy to say this. Her lip trembled and her eyes filled with tears, in spite of herself.

'What will you do?' he said, his ruddy face paling a little; and his voice shook in spite of himself as he asked the question.

'Do? We must do what we can,' said Madge, trying to smile. 'Molly has had a better education than I have; she will go out as a governess; and I—I should like to be a nurse.'

She sighed as she spoke, and her hands dropped by her side, and her eyes brimmed over.

'A nurse?' he repeated. 'Are you sure that you are strong enough and brave enough for a nurse?'

'It is all I can do,' said Madge sadly. 'I am not of very much use. I have no accomplishments; but I could nurse the sick. I have nursed my father and my mother and the children in all their illnesses; and I think, besides, I have nursed nearly all the old men and women in the village. I may want method; but I do not want experience.'

She tried her hardest to keep the tears back, but they would fall.

'I think you are quite right,' he said. 'I think you have made the right choice. I am sure you are well fitted for the work you have chosen. So dutiful a daughter, so tender a sister, cannot but make the best nurse for the sick and the afflicted. If you will let me, I will make inquiries for you. You will require skilled training, and I will find out what hospital would be best for you.'

And so, with this promise, he went away.

He didn't say anything about finding a situation for Molly.

This offer of looking out for a hospital gave him very frequent opportunities of writing to Madge and hearing all particulars of the movements of the girls. But what puzzled Molly so much during this miserable time was that, instead of her sister looking woebegone and fretting her eyes out, as she had every excuse for doing, she went about all the trying work that fell to her lot with a strange light in her eyes and a pink spot on her cheek that Molly never remembered to have seen there before.

She had never told her younger sister about that earlier acquaintance with David Llewelyn, nor of the question he had asked her one day, when, like his last visit now, he had come to say good-bye. He had not asked her the same question this time. He had only said that he would look out for a hospital.

How Madge could go about all that terrible work of sorting, laying aside, and packing up, without breaking down every minute, puzzled Molly. She could not trust herself to disturb anything in those sacred drawers in her father's study; she could not turn out the big hanging press that had been locked when her mother died, and was full of old-fashioned gowns that she could but dimly remember clinging to with her childish fingers. It was like opening a vault and looking upon the forgotten face of the dead.

It seemed such profanity to her, prying into these things, so long treasured as relics, and asking helplessly, 'What shall we do with them?'

Something had to be done with them, and it had to be done without delay, for the day of the sale was fixed, and the days and the weeks flew by so quickly that when the auctioneer's men were already in the house the packing was still undone.

Madge was quite a marvel to her sister in those last days. She did all the necessary painful things without breaking down, and with a grave, settled calmness of manner that nothing could disturb. It seemed quite heroic to Molly; but, then, she had no one to sustain her drooping spirits with nice sympathizing letters at least twice a week, even though the ostensible subject was but the choice of a hospital.

There was no one to write any words of comfort to Molly but Dorothy Piggott. Adela had nothing to write about but the things she had left behind, and she filled whole pages on this interesting subject.

They packed up her things and sent them to her at her Aunt Gray's house at Cambridge, with whom she proposed to stay for the present. She had only another term at

Newnham before her Tripos, and after that she was to be married. Happy, happy Adela !

Nobody ever mentioned the Junior Dean's name now ; indeed, he was Junior Dean no longer. He had resigned his office and gone away—no one quite knew where. It was rumoured to some crowded London parish. He might have written, Molly thought, to her sister when he heard of their bereavement, and expressed some sorrow or sympathy with their loss, but he had made no sign. And Jack had not been heard of since that winter day when he shouldered his bag and went through the snow with Peter following at his heels.

The girls ought to have left the neighbourhood before the sale. It seemed a cruel and unnecessary trial to remain on the spot and see their home dismantled and carried away bit by bit. It appeared, however, that it could not be helped. The surveyor appointed by the Ecclesiastical Commissioners to assess the dilapidations could not come until the day after the sale. He could not see, he explained, the state of the walls until the furniture was removed. The panelling might be, and probably was, quite rotten.

A kind neighbour who occupied a farm adjoining the Rectory took the girls in, and made them as comfortable as she could, giving up to them her best bedroom that commanded a view of the village street, from whence they could see the people trooping up and down to the sale.

They did not leave the Rectory until the dusk was falling on the previous night. And then, when the auctioneer's men were gone, they went through the house together for the last time. On the morrow the things would be all dispersed, and it would be 'home' no longer. It was like taking a last farewell of the dying. They would never see the familiar faces of the things they had looked upon all their lives again. Someone else would sit in their father's chair; other children would gather round the big dining-table; other faces would be reflected back by the old mirrors. The books they had read, the games they had played, the ferns they had reared so carefully, would belong to others.

It was past thinking of; the sight of the dear old shabby things, with a nasty white ticket stuck upon them, brought a rush of tears to Molly's eyes. It was worse than giving up the house in Cambridge. She loathed those little dandy plush chairs she had bought with so much pride for her new home; and she loved these old shabby things, with the torn coverings and the horsehair sticking out.

Perhaps the cruellest cut of all was passing out across the lawn, where the outdoor things were on view.

It was a collection of rubbish, and would probably be sold for a song; but the sight of it went to Molly's heart with a sharp pain, like a knife in a green wound.

There was the wheelbarrow Jack used to drive her in when she was a child; the old lawn-mower they had so often pulled over the grass together; the rusty garden tools they had used as children; the hutches where Jack kept his rabbits; the cage where the ferret lived; the box he made for his white mice. Everything had a voice and a memory. The croquet set, and the tennis net, and the shabby old racquets, recalled those happy, happy days that would never come again.

Molly turned from them with a bursting heart and the tears running down her face—but they did not move Madge.

'I must say good-bye to Merrylegs,' said Molly when they reached the Rectory gate. She had forgotten the old gray pony in the stable—she had seen so little of him since her return. She left her sister at the gate and ran down the path to the stables. Merrylegs heard the familiar step, and whinnied before she opened the door.

He came over, as he had done ever since she could remember, and put his old gray nose in her hand, in search of the accustomed biscuit. But there was no biscuit to-day.

'Oh, you poor old dear!' she sobbed, with her arms around his neck, and the tears running down his rough coat. 'I shall never, never see you again! I hope whoever has you will be good to you; but you must be true to your old friends, Merrylegs; you must never love anybody but me and Jack!'

She kissed his old gray face and shut the door, and hurried up the path, but there was yet another claimant for her notice. The kennel had been carried on to the lawn, and the old yard-dog was straining himself to the verge of suicide at the end of his chain to reach her. He had been given to Jack when a puppy, and had been his faithful humble friend ever since. Molly went over and patted him, and he made her new black dress in a dreadful mess with his paws.

'Down, Rover! dear fellow! Good-bye, Rover! Oh, good-bye! good-bye, Rover!'

# CHAPTER XXXIX.

## MOLLY'S QUIXOTISM.

'O death in life, the days that are no more.'

THE partings were over, and the sale was over. There was nothing to be done but to go through the house with the surveyor, who came to assess the dilapidations.

The late Rector had held the living so many years, and had done so little to the Rectory house internally, that it was just possible the valuation might be high. The roofs and the walls were in good repair, and watertight, but the interior of the house, when all the furniture was removed, looked dreadfully out of repair.

The girls acknowledged it with a sigh, as the surveyor went poking about the rooms, and making rapid notes in a book he carried. He wasn't content with making notes of the apparent condition of the rooms; he carried a stick and poked it viciously into the woodwork to try if it were rotten; and if that were not effectual he kicked it with his iron-heeled boot, and sometimes the panels gave way, and the boot went through.

It went to the heart of the two girls looking on. It seemed wanton cruelty. It was the dismallest work they had yet done, going through those empty rooms, that were haunted with such happy memories, with that stony-hearted surveyor and his inexorable boot.

The furniture that had not been cleared away stood outside round the front door as they came in. They had no idea until they saw it in the crucial light of day how old and mean and shabby it was. There was Molly's dressing-table, that used to look so dainty in its muslin covering, standing in the middle of the path, looking indescribably shabby, and the old glass that for so many years had reflected her bright face. It would reflect someone else's face now.

They hurried past all these familiar things with a shiver ; but the house itself—the poor old empty house—was shabbier and meaner than even the old dressing-table and the glass. It was full of strange echoes and sounds, as the March wind swept through the open doors and through the dismantled rooms, like the voices of the dead.

There were strange shapes on the walls where the furniture and the pictures and the glasses had once stood or hung — eerie outlines of things that had once been ; but these were nothing to the unsubstantial shadows that thronged the empty rooms.

Here, where that cruel man was making his

rapid notes, they had gathered for meals, and had knelt morning and evening ever since they could remember. They forgot the man and his notes—at least, Molly did—and subsided into a passion of tears on the narrow window-ledge. There was nowhere else to sit ; there wasn't a chair in the place. There was only the bare floor, and she couldn't sit on the floor and cry.

And then, as if to add insult to injury, the man came over and requested her to move, that he might examine the casement. He shook it with such force that it was a wonder that every pane of glass didn't drop out ; and when it had stood that ordeal he made a malicious little note that the fastening was out of order.

And so he went through the house, poking at all the woodwork, rattling all the window-sashes, and putting all the locks through inquisitorial tests.

Molly couldn't stand it any longer. She

sank down sobbing on that narrow windowledge when he had left the room, and begged Madge to take her away. They could do no good by staying; they could not move him one inch. Their presence only seemed to provoke him to more heartless investigations.

They left him to his task, and hurried through the little crowd at the front door, and down through the path, where the people were carrying away all the familiar things. Their last memory of their old house was the man poking at the woodwork, and the shabby old dressing-table on the lawn, and a crippled couch being borne along the path before them with the horsehair sticking out.

They went away the same day. They went to London, travelling third class in a crowded train with a lot of market people. Molly cried all the way behind her veil. She put on a veil for the first time in her life that morning. It seemed to shut her and her grief out from the common world. She would never go out without one again, she told herself. For one thing, she would have grown so perfectly hideous with her red nose and her swollen eyes that she wouldn't be fit to be seen.

But she was quite fit to be seen the next morning, when Mr. Llewelyn called at their lodgings to take the sisters to the hospital he had selected for them. It had come to that at last—that Molly had thrown over all her Newnham education, and had decided to be a nurse.

She was weak in her classics and uncertain in her mathematics, although she had managed to pull through one part of the Little-go. She wasn't at all sure that she could teach anything perfectly; but she could nurse the sick and comfort the dying. The experience of that one dying bed was so burnt into her heart and brain that it had changed the aspect of everything. There was a different meaning in all the common things of life—in all the sights and sounds of nature.

The message used to be life and love once; it was love still—but love and death. And so, with the message ringing in her ears, and all the brightness slipping out of her life, Molly decided to become a nurse.

She didn't get much encouragement in her decision—not even from Mr. Llewelyn, who had said such nice things about Madge. Adela thought it was the height of folly— sheer quixotism. Even Mrs. Gray wrote a very mild letter, begging her to reconsider her determination, and not to throw away all those advantages she had gained at Newnham.

Only Dorothy Piggott wrote her a dear little letter commending her resolve, and hinting that, at some future day, she might follow her example. She was going through with her Tripos. The honour of the college was at stake, and she would do her best for the sake of Newnham—dear Newnham !

There was a little note of sadness running through her letter ; there was none of the old elation in it. Had the Black Ox trodden upon Dorothy Piggott's toes as well as upon her own ? Molly asked herself, as she read her friend's letter. Had Mr. Brackenbury proved false ?

A strange thing happened soon after the girls came to London. A letter reached them, forwarded from Silverton, addressed to Jack. Letters for Jack were not unusual, but they were of a well-recognised type, and bore a monotonous family likeness. They were generally bills from Cambridge tradesmen.

'Another bill of Jack's !' said Madge wearily, tossing the letter aside, and beginning to read, with a heightened colour, another letter that came by the same post. She had received a good many letters in the same hand lately; they were only about hospitals, but they never failed to bring a flush to her pale cheeks.

But Jack's letter was not a bill. It was in a square envelope, and it was not in the painfully legible handwriting peculiar to bills. Molly thought she knew the writing. The sight of it brought back the old Cambridge days; and Jack's old room seemed to rise up before her, and the college teas she used to preside over, and the untrustworthy tea-kettle, and the face of Mr. Brackenbury bending over it.

The letter was from Mr. Brackenbury. She was quite sure of it, before her sister opened it.

Molly would have put it in the fire unopened; she grew hot and angry whenever she thought of Mr. Brackenbury, and the sight of his letter sent quite a shiver through her. Madge was more practical. 'We can burn it just as well after we've read it,' she said, and she opened the letter.

Molly had guessed correctly ; the letter was from Mr. Brackenbury, and it contained a cheque for two hundred and fifty pounds.

'I had forgotten all about that bill,' he wrote : 'I'm awfully sorry. I hope it didn't matter much. Do you remember the Romney I sent to Christie's ? The old woman fetched a thousand ! I send you a fourth of the spoil as my share in the bill.'

It was only common honesty on the part of Mr. Brackenbury, and the money really belonged to the girls ; it was part of their father's estate.

He had paid the money, Jack's share and Mr. Brackenbury's share, and the repayment was due. But nothing could induce Molly to take that view of the case. She would have thrown the cheque in the fire if Madge hadn't taken it from her hands.

'He has killed papa and he has ruined Jack ; he has brought all this trouble upon us—he has spoilt our lives; and now he insults us with a paltry cheque ! not one word of honest regret, not one thought or care for the misery he has wrought ! Oh, Madge! we will not keep his money ; it will bring a curse with it. Let us send it back at once. I could not sleep with it in the house.'

Molly was very much in earnest ; her nostrils were dilated, her eyes very hard and bright, and her small head proud and erect.

'I don't think we have any right to throw away the money,' said Madge humbly. 'It belongs to papa—to us ; it is only the payment of a just debt—and if Jack should return it would belong to him.'

It was this argument that decided Molly.

'Let him keep it, then,' she said, 'till Jack comes. I would not take charge of it for the world !'

She sat down at once, and wrote her first and last letter to Mr. Brackenbury :

'I return your cheque,' she wrote; 'it has come too late. My brother is lost, and my father has broken his heart. You have ruined my brother's life—you have ruined mine. God forgive you, for I cannot.

'MARY GRAY.'


She felt better after she had written this letter; and, while the mood was on her, she wrote another to Dorothy Piggott. She told her the whole story—the bare, naked truth—the miserable story of her brother's connection with Mr. Brackenbury, and the ruin it had caused.

Though it was raining hard, and no one would have turned a dog into the streets on such a night, she insisted on going out to post these letters herself before she went to bed.

The result of her quixotism was that she got wet through, and was laid up with a cold for the next week.

The very next morning Madge had cause to regret this act of folly. The Ecclesiastical Commissioners sent in their assessment for dilapidations. It was over four hundred pounds.

There was no appeal against it : there was no possible redress. It would quite swallow up the total amount of the sale, and trench upon the insurance. Mr. Brackenbury's cheque could not have been applied to a better purpose. It would not have burnt the fingers of the Ecclesiastical Commissioners, and they would have had no compunctions about accepting it.

Madge was quite right when she declared that it was an act of pure quixotism.

Mr. David Llewelyn, when he was told of it—and Madge could not keep anything from him for her life—took a different view of the matter. 'I don't think your sister could have done anything else,' he said, 'feeling as she did in the matter. I think I should have done the same.'

Very few people have a chance of being quixotic more than once in a lifetime, but to Molly the opportunity again presented itself. It was not till a year after that sad exodus. A great deal had happened in that intervening year. In the ceaseless anxious work, and care, and thought for others, something like the low beginnings of content had come to her.

She had found, as so many have found, in unselfish work for others something more satisfying than happiness. She had seen all her early hopes die out; all the promise and hope of a bright untroubled future fade before her eyes. She had sadly watched it all go, melt quite away, and yet it was not all loss she felt. A new call that spoke of a higher and a stronger task had opened out before her. She had lost much in the year that had gone, but she had gained more.

She had lost something of that beauty and brightness that dazzled everybody. Her eyes were softer and fuller of thought, and her face was grave and settled. The simple nurse's dress set it off to perfection.

It seemed, indeed, to have been invented as the most fitting frame for sweet, thoughtful faces. A great many young doctors have doubtless thought the same. Several doctors at the hospital where Molly spent her year of probation had held the same opinion, and more than one had asked her to exchange it for another dress, not so becoming, but more befitting the position to which he proposed to transplant her. To all of these young men Molly had but one answer; and her face was graver and her eyes were steadier after each of these refusals. They would have been brighter in the old time, and she would have made merry over her victims; but suffering had taught her to be considerate to the feelings of others, to give no needless pain.

Her year of probation was quite over, and she was talking with her sister in a recess of one of the hospital wards, looking out of the window into the quiet court below. It was the last night of the sisters being under the same roof. They had worked together, if not in the same wards, in the same building all the year; they had not been separated for a single night. Something was about to happen on the morrow, and one of them would never, after to-night, sleep under that roof again.

Madge was smiling and soft-eyed, and yet her cheeks were wet with tears; but Molly's face was graver even than usual, and her eyes were settled and calm.

'I have only one trouble, Molly,' said the elder sister, with a suspicious catch in her voice, ' and that is leaving you.'

'You needn't make that a trouble, dear,' said Molly with a smile; her voice was quieter and softer, like her eyes. 'We should have been separated soon, in any case. I, too, have made my choice. I am going away. Not like you, to a sweet country parish, with the dearest and best husband in the world' (here the elder sister's eyes brimmed over, and she broke down with a little sob). 'I am going, Heaven only knows where—wherever it sends me—to do the work that I have been training for, oh! so blindly, all these years. I have found my vocation at last, Madge.'

'Your vocation ! What are you going to do, Molly ?'

'I don't know yet, dear, what I am going to do. The work will be found for me. I only know, whatever it may be, I will do it with my whole heart!'

'Oh, Molly, it's something quixotic!'

It was the old cry; but Molly didn't smile. There was a light shining in her eyes, but they were not smiling.

'Yes,' she said softly, 'I suppose people will call it quixotic. Adela will, and Aunt Gray; but I don't think Keith would, or Jack, or papa, if he can look down from his happy place and see his wee girlie.'

Her eyes were full of tears now; but the light shone still beneath them. It was the first time that Madge had heard her mention her lover's name; it seemed to have slipped out unawares in that moment of exaltation.

'What are you going to do, darling? I am sure you will never do anything unworthy,' said Madge anxiously.

'Not going to do, dear; I have already done it. I have offered myself to the Zenana Society—and they have accepted me. I am going wherever they send me.'

'Oh. Molly ! you have done this without consulting me !'

'Where was the use, dear ? You would have been sure to say " No." I have no tie like you, Madge, to hold me back. I have no duty in life to keep me here. It is only single-minded, single-hearted women who are wanted. I am single-hearted, God knows ! And—and I have no one in the world to keep me back !'

Here Molly broke down, and wept a few small tears on her sister's bosom. She wept a few more the next day, when Madge stood in a sober travelling dress trembling before the altar in an unpretending London church.

It was a very quiet wedding. There was no one but the old clerk to give the bride away, and Molly, in her nurse's garb, was the only bridesmaid.

The sisters parted at the church door ; but

Madge was too happy to shed many tears, and she had, oh, such a commonplace husband! It was the *locum tenens* that she had sent away so heartlessly many years ago, and that turned up so unexpectedly in their time of need.

He had nothing to recommend him but his faithful, manly heart, and a living of two hundred and fifty pounds a year; but Madge was as foolishly happy and radiant as if she had married the Archbishop of Canterbury.

Adela had been married for several months; but her wedding had been a very different affair. She had taken a first-class in the Classical Tripos, and she had married the master of a college. Her sisters had not been present at the wedding, which had been graced by the presence of a Vice-Chancellor and a Vice-Chancelloress, and half the dons and donesses in Cambridge.

It had been a most brilliant affair, and

Mrs. Gray, from whose house her niece was married, had worn on the occasion a new satin gown of her favourite colour.

The bride, in consideration of her father's recent death and the advanced age of the bridegroom, who was a widower, had appeared at the altar, not in girlish white, but in the tenderest and softest shade of mauve—pensive, delicate mauve—and Mrs. Gray had extinguished it completely with her gorgeous toilet of brilliant magenta.

She was so good as to send her nieces, along with the bride-cake, a pattern of each of the wedding gowns. Madge laughed when she took them out of the wrapper till she cried. She was going to be married herself shortly, and the sight of wedding garments affected her. Molly neither laughed nor cried, but the sight of that magenta gown afforded her the most solid satisfaction.

# CHAPTER XL.

### A RIFT IN THE CLOUDS.

> ' The new day comes the light
> Dearer for night, as dearer thou for faults
> Lived over——'

THE Rev. Keith Fellowes—he was a Junior Dean no longer—had not been idle during all these weary months. He had been working hard, for one thing, in a densely-populated London parish—a solitary curate among a population of ten thousand, all poor.

He had not forgotten during all these toilsome days, among these squalid surroundings, that happy dream that had once held such a foremost place in his life. He had heard from time to time of Molly. He had heard of Jack's disappearance, of her father's death, of the breaking up of her home. He had heard of all these things befalling the woman he loved— he had never wavered in his love for her all these years; what good man ever wavers in his love for a good woman?—and he had done the only thing that was left for him to do, as blow after blow fell on that dear head— he had prayed for her through all.

He had heard of her work as a hospital nurse, and he had thanked God for it. In the simplicity of his heart he had told himself that this was a distinct answer to prayer— his prayer—and so he had gone on praying.

And then suddenly a cloud, darker than any cloud that had yet fallen upon his path, came between him and the sun, and the familiar name faltered upon his lips. Word had been brought him from the hospital that the nurse's place was vacant—that Molly Gray was married.

He was not quite sure that he ought to go on praying for another man's wife; but he was sure of one thing, that he must give up his work and go away. There was nothing now to detain him in London. So long as the girl he loved was here, and was engaged in kindred work, he could have stayed on for ever.

Now everything was changed, and there was nothing to detain him. He resigned his charge without delay, and went over the same afternoon to Islington, and offered himself to the Church Missionary Society.

It is not often that the society has the offer of a senior theologian—the Church at home has bigger prizes to offer than an ill-paid, hard-worked missionary church—and if they didn't exactly jump at him, they accepted his offer.

There was a missionary party going out the following month, and they pressed him to join it. The post of president of a training college for native pastors in North India was vacant, and the committee were unanimous in urging it upon his acceptance.

It was not exactly the missionary work Keith Fellowes had set his heart upon, but it was a post of usefulness; and, perhaps, with his lame foot, it was better suited for him than the jungles of Central Africa.

Before he went he revisited his old friends at Cambridge. He had left his books and various things behind at his old rooms. His ostensible purpose, he told himself, was to pack up his books; but before he left his native shores he had a strange yearning to see once more the spot that had been sacred to his short-lived happiness. It was for Molly's sake—even so; though lost to him, it was for her sake he undertook that visit to Cambridge.

There were very few people who recognised him as he walked through the busy streets.

The world had gone on just the same without him ; he hadn't even left any debts behind him to be remembered by.

There were new names over most of the doors; there were new faces in the courts; another Fellow was occupying his old rooms, and a new Junior Dean was reading the service in his college chapel.

He had dropped quite out of the old life here, and he hadn't been missed.

Mr. Flynt welcomed him more warmly than the rest of the Fellows, and congratulated him on the step he had taken. 'It was in the way of promotion ; and—well, great things might follow by-and-by. It was a position quite worthy of a senior theologian and a Fellow of St. Stephen's.'

The only person who seemed really glad to see him was a little scholar of the college that he remembered in his freshman's year. He came out of the staircase where Jack had once kept, as he was passing, and he ran up to him and shook hands with him, and asked for news of Jack.

'I am sorry to say I know nothing of him,' said Keith Fellowes with a sigh—he was thinking of Molly and her trouble. 'His friends have not heard from him since he went away.'

'Not heard from him since he went away!' said little Blantyre in a tone of concern. 'I'm awfully sorry. I hoped it had all been made up. Gray was the best friend I ever had. He saved me from losing my scholarship, that first term when — when Mr. Brackenbury squibbed the senior tutor; and he saved all the college being sent down when there was that row about the chapel window. Gray was innocent of both these things, but because the other fellow was a sneak, he took the blame on himself that the innocent shouldn't suffer for the guilty. I have heard from him once since he went away; he was roughing it in the Bush. He had gone through a good deal, I should think, by his letter. He was cattle-driving when he wrote. He didn't say much about himself; he wrote to thank me for a little dog I had given him when he went away. He had taken it with him, and it had been a great comfort to him. He didn't know what he should have done, he said, without Peter.'

Jack's case was not an uncommon one. There are plenty of University men knocking about Australia—men who have in their own lives repeated the traditional story of the fall; committed the old blunders; stumbled into the old temptations; and awoke up, generally too late, to the old dismay.

But Keith Fellowes was not thinking about Jack; he was thinking about Molly, as he wandered through the familiar courts and loitered about the old spots. He stood in the twilight on the college bridge, where they had so often stood together; and as he stood there, a faint blue mist crept up from the river and veiled all the gray sad distance; and when he turned to go away, the crescent moon rose above the mist and cast a silver radiance on his path.

There was nothing to keep him in Cambridge, and he went down the next day.

A week after that hurried visit he stood on the deck of the P. and O. steamer that was to carry him away to the scene of his future labours. There was quite a large party of fellow missionaries on the ship, men and women, and the leave-takings had been something dreadful. He had nobody to take leave of: there was no one among that crowd on the shore that was shedding a single tear for him, and yet he was quite unnerved.

He stood apart from the group of weeping women, and the men who were almost as deeply moved, as they took a farewell—to so many a last farewell—of the stricken watchers on the shore. He turned away from the acute agony of the eyes straining to catch a last look at the slowly receding faces, for the vessel had let go her moorings, and was steaming out of dock.

There were no tearful eyes straining for him, but he could not bear the sight; his heart melted within him—as if he had a wife and six children all reaching out their arms to him from the shore—and the name of the woman he loved rose to his lips.

He thought of Molly as he watched the crowd on the quay melt away, and the white cliffs and the sweet English landscape fade slowly from his eyes.

He was still thinking of her, when someone began to quaver out the first line of a hymn—

'God be with you till we meet again!'

It was a very trying hymn to sing with

everyone weeping around him, and the voices quavered and faltered in a most unusual way.

They broke down at the end of the first verse, and it was hopeless to think of going on. There was a solemn pause, broken only by the sobbing of the women, and the men uncovered their heads and prayed silently for those they had left behind.

A mist came before Keith Fellowes' eyes, and the dear name of the woman he loved was on his lips. He turned aside to hide his emotion; he hadn't seen the face of any one of his fellow labourers, and he couldn't see clearly now through the mist, but the first face he did see, in the little noble group of men and women who were going out at the Master's call to toil, and pain, and suffering— and death perhaps—was the face of the dear woman whose name was on his lips.

The clouds all rolled away during that long

tranquil journey, and in the shining path of duty and unselfish work that lay before them, Molly and her lover saw no shadow of another parting.

Mr. Flynt's words were prophetic. Promotion had come when least expected, and Keith Fellowes' next visit to Cambridge was to receive the well-merited distinction of a doctor's degree conferred by his old University.

Adela's husband happened to fill the Vice-Chancellor's chair on this occasion, but, rheumaticky as he was in his joints, he had to rise from it to confer the degree of Doctor of Divinity on his brother-in-law.

According to University etiquette a Vice-Chancellor must rise to his peers, and Keith Fellowes had recently been ordained the youngest Bishop on the bench.

Oh, what a proud and happy day it was for Molly! She nearly broke down when the new doctor came over in his scarlet gown, and took his seat beside her in the doctors' gallery of the Senate House.

Adela behaved beautifully, and was a most charming hostess, and the most devoted of sisters.

Truly, nothing succeeds like success!

We must make one exception in favour of a patent medicine. It does not matter whether it is a pill or a potion; whether to be taken internally or applied externally. It is not even necessary to name it. It was on every tongue, it was echoed (in monster letters) by every wall in Cambridge. The advertisement columns of the local papers were full of it.

It was talked about in Cambridge a great deal more than the new Bishop. A caravan emblazoned with illustrations of miraculous cures drove through the streets to the blatant music of a brass band, and conveyed the great benefactor, who had discovered this wonderful remedy, to the market-place, where he expatiated at certain hours of the day to a listening crowd on its virtues.

The new Bishop happened to be passing one day when the benefactor was holding forth, from the front of the caravan, on the virtues of the nostrum that he sold.

Something in the voice arrested his attention. It was not the voice of a street orator; it was not the voice of a mountebank. It was a clear, perfectly modulated voice. It was the voice of culture and refinement; and he had certainly heard it before.

The crowd was not only listening; it was hanging upon every word. It swayed the great concourse of people that filled the market-place like one man. They could not withstand that delightful voice. Their shillings and their sixpences tumbled in like a shower.

Keith Fellowes pressed into the middle of the crowd, where he looked dreadfully out of place, if anyone had been looking; but nobody had eyes to spare for a mere Bishop.

The face of the speaker was as familiar as his voice. A pale, pensive, clean-shaven face, with long black hair falling over the collar of his Spanish-looking jacket.

The get-up was bizarre and striking, resembling the dress of a Spanish matador at a bull-fight; but the most effective part of it was the great soft brigand-looking hat that threw the pale pensive face into deep shadow.

The new Bishop was quite sure he had seen the face before. He had seen so many faces in his time that he could not recall it, and he was turning away when the orator raised his hat.

He took it off with a flourish, and bade his audience adieu, until the performance should be resumed at a later hour.

There was a mockery in his politeness to the foolish gaping crowd, a demure irrepressible twinkle in his eyes which revealed his identity.

It was Mr. Brackenbury.

Keith Fellowes turned away in disgust; he had heard all that sad story of Jack's from Molly, and the sight of this man, who had given her so much pain, was hateful to him.

As he pushed his way through the crowd a carriage drove up; a tawdry carriage with piebald horses, and glittering harness, and bells tinkling.

There was only one occupant, a showily-dressed woman with a beautiful weary face. The crowd cheered her, as she sat unheeding, waiting for the mountebank at the edge of the crowd. She did not smile when he got in; she did not even look his way; she lay back in the tawdry carriage, with a weary look on her beautiful, dissatisfied face.

The Bishop flushed as scarlet as his new gown, and trembled, actually trembled all over.

It was Rosey.

He went home and told Molly all about it. There were no secrets between them now.

'Oh dear!' said Molly, 'what an escape for Dorothy Piggott!'

It *was* an escape for Dorothy Piggott, who at the present moment was the head of a woman's college, while her old lover was a mountebank selling quack nostrums in the market-place.

THE END.

BILLING AND SONS, PRINTERS, GUILDFO RD.

www.ingramcontent.com/pod-product-compliance
Lightning Source LLC
Chambersburg PA
CBHW032105220426
43664CB00008B/1143